five-minute
mysteries

DATE DUE

five-minute
mysteries

40
additional
cases
of
murder
and
mayhem
for
you
to
solve

5

ken weber

FIREFLY BOOKS

A FIREFLY BOOK

Published by Firefly Books Ltd., 2005

First Printing 2005

National Library of Canada Cataloguing in Publication

Weber, K. J. (Kenneth Jerome), 1940–
Five-minute mysteries 5 : 40 additional cases
of murder and mayhem for you to solve / Ken Weber.
ISBN 1-55297-868-0
1. Detective and mystery stories, Canadian (English) 2. Literary recreations.
3. Puzzles. I. Title.
GV1507.D4W455 2005   793.73   C2005-901186-6

Published in Canada in 2005 by
Firefly Books Ltd.
66 Leek Crescent
Richmond Hill, Ontario L4B 1H1

Design: HotHouse Canada
Printed and bound in Canada

*The publisher gratefully acknowledges the financial support for our
publishing program by the Canada Council for the Arts, the Ontario
Arts Council and the Government of Canada through the Book
Publishing Industry Development Program.*

For Matthew, Cameron, Aiden and Finn

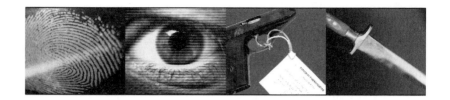

Unsolved Cases

Memorandum

To: ALL MYSTERY BUFFS
From: the author

Mystery buffs know there are only two kinds of people in the world: those who love mysteries and, well, that other kind. A tiny majority, the latter are, and that's a good thing because they are missing something unique. For only in mysteries can a reader get a charge out of winning or losing.

It works like this. Nothing gives mystery buffs more satisfaction than getting ahead in a story and beating the writer to the punch. They get a special charge out of combining logic, analysis, intuition and insight so that before they turn the last page, they already have the problem solved. Yet — and this is what sets mystery lovers apart — nothing thrills them more than when the mystery defeats them, when they turn the last page and find a surprise waiting, something they'd missed.

In this, the fifth installment of the series, mystery lovers get no less than forty shots at the fun of winning or losing, in a set of wildly different stories. Every mystery in the book is set up for the reader to solve. At the end of each mystery there is a question: *Who did …?* or *What did …?* or *It seems the thief made a mistake. How could …?* Like that.

There's great variety. The settings range from city to country, from a bank to a beach, and from France to Australia. You'll encounter detectives, thieves and murderers, a sub-lieutenant searching for deserters during the Napoleonic Wars, an undercover KGB agent and a centurion in the Roman Empire.

There's also variety in the level of challenge. As you turn the pages of **Five-minute Mysteries 5** you'll notice one, two or three symbols — a gun — at the beginning of each story. The number of guns suggests how easy or difficult the mystery is, one being easy, two being a little harder, and three, difficult. (Or, perhaps more accurately, how easy or difficult each one seems to me.) But don't let the ratings stop you from enjoying all the mysteries! One that I rate "difficult" might be an open-and-shut case for you, while you might be utterly stumped by one I've rated "easy." Try them all.

Finally, all the solutions are at the back of the book, so you can prove you're a winner or, once in a while, get a kick out of losing. Either way, enjoy.

Alone on the Beach

Tony Sanchez lowered himself to one knee beside the body, being very careful not to touch the footprints in the sand. There were two sets of these, one of them obviously made by the little man in the chair, the dead man. His prints were smooth, like the soles of his expensive dress shoes and, consistent with the weight of the man, the indentations in the sand were very shallow. Had there been more beach traffic, they might not have been seen at all.

"Good thing it's off season." The voice came from behind Tony, echoing his thoughts. "Nobody in the cabins. Snack shack's closed. Only people on the whole beach last night were the runt here and whoever popped 'im."

Even if he hadn't recognized the voice instantly, Tony would have clued in from the attitude of the speaker. Manny Silver, Tony's temporary partner on the Biloxi homicide squad, had several reprimands in his personnel file citing his disrespect for victims of crime and their survivors. As far as Tony was concerned, in the two months they had worked together, there had been no evidence of moderation in Silver's style.

Tony got to his feet slowly and turned right around so he could look his partner full in the face.

"I *know* this man," he said.

"You know the … the vic?" Manny was genuinely surprised. Biloxi's territory was not a large one but this didn't happen often for, as in most tourist areas, a large percentage of the population was transient.

"A friend of yours?" Manny was backpedaling. Tony was not only his senior and two grades up in rank, he had a reputation as a completely no-nonsense cop.

"He lives in my building and no, he's not a friend but I know him. Everybody in the building knows him — knew him. He was different. Not odd really but, well, *unusual*. Hard to miss."

Manny sensed an opportunity for a fresh start. "Yea, that's for sure!" He moved around to the other side of the large wooden beach chair that seemed so far out of proportion to the man it held. "I mean, how many people do you know that walk on the beach with a fancy cane? And Oxfords? But then come to think of it, if you wear a vest and a whaddayacallit — cravat? — and a suit, you're not just another dude, you're … you're … well, let's face it, Tony, you gotta be just a bit *strange!*"

Tony didn't respond but instead angled himself farther from the victim, keeping to the same side of the chair. From the new position he had a clearer front view of the dead man. Were it not for the bullet hole in his chest — and the clothes — the little man might have passed for just another tourist walking the beach who sat down for a rest and fell asleep. But there were too many factors slicing through that impression, the most striking of which was the blood and the wood splinters on the sand behind the chair. It struck Tony as more than a bit ironic, almost — he hated to think it: *appropriate* — that this meticulously dressed man would be shot by someone using a carefully chosen bullet that barely disturbed his appearance on entering the chest, but blew a mighty exit hole on the way out, taking chunks of the chair back with it.

He finally spoke. "We called him Mr. Micawber, the people in our building did. Partly it was the little tummy sticking out and him being so short. See how the footprints come up to the chair and when he sits his feet don't touch the ground?"

"Yea, looks like he died without ever getting out of the chair again."

Tony didn't seem to be aware of the interruption. "And the formal dress. He always wore a three-piece suit, starched collars, a hat and cane. Come to think of it, I don't see a hat anywhere. We've got to check into that. May be something to it."

Manny Silver rotated a full circle. "Yea, no hat anywhere I can see. So was this Mick-whatever — he's Irish or something, is he? — was he in the habit of walking on the beach this early in the morning?"

"I don't know if he's Irish or not. It's not Mick in that sense. Mr. Micawber was a character in *David Copperfield*."

"This guy worked for Copperfield? The magician?"

Tony was silent as he contemplated his response. "The novel by Charles Dickens," he said finally. "In *David Copperfield* there's a popular character who always dressed up like he was well off, even when he wasn't."

If Manny was even slightly embarrassed by the gap in his literary background, he concealed it admirably. "So could be our vic here was hard up. Closet gambler maybe with big debts? Might be a motive there."

"I have no idea at all about his finances," Tony replied. "All I know is what I've told you. Except that the women all thought he was wonderful."

"Aw, women always like short guys, 'specially when they're old. Means they're sure to be harmless."

"No, that's not it. It's because he was so polite. A total gentleman in every way. My wi ... my ex always used to say he should give lessons."

"Awright, so we got mister supermanners with the weird clothes goes for a walk on the beach and gets himself blown away by..." Manny went down on one knee just as Tony had on the other side of the chair. "He gets himself blown away by somebody wearing — uh, wearing..." He bent over to the second set of footprints that led to the chair, leaning so close to them that his nose almost touched. "Wearing a pair of ladies' New Balance, 7½ double D, I'd say."

Manny stood and grinned at the expression on Tony's face. "I used to work in a shoe store. You get good at the sizes in a hurry." He put his hands on his hips. "So. My take is the vic, Mr. Mi*caw*ber, is out for his constitutional. Very early morning. Beach is deserted. He sits in the chair here and Ms. New Balance, 7½ double D, walks up — you can see where she stands and shifts a bit — puts one through the vest and then walks away. Just one, two, three, like that. You agree?"

Tony nodded, paused, and then nodded again. "Except for one thing," he said. "I say the shooter was a guy."

Manny frowned. "Yea? What makes you say that?"

What makes Tony Sanchez say that?

Solution on page 172

Border Alert

2

The call came in from the RCMP at 4:11 p.m. Larkin had begun her shift at 4 p.m., and over the eleven minutes she had passed three passenger cars through her checkpoint. That was normal traffic for a Wednesday afternoon in late August, as the border crossing where Larkin worked was a quiet one, even on holiday weekends. To the north, Quebec's Highway 55 stretched up to the town of Magog and west to Montreal. To the south, U.S. Interstate 91 reached into Vermont and beyond. On both sides of the border, the area was rural and densely forested.

The RCMP's alert had been followed by one from the FBI only seconds later and both gave similar, very limited information: a suspected terrorist would be attempting to cross the border some time before 6 p.m. The only really useful information the two agencies added was that the suspect was definitely male and that they were 80 percent to 90 percent certain he was Caucasian. The RCMP's alert stated that the subject may (like every other customs officer, Larkin snorted at the "may") have greasy or grimy hands for there was evidence — once more with 80 percent to 90 percent certainty — that he was an auto mechanic. From the FBI came information that the subject may have a bushy, dark mustache.

By 4:12, Larkin's supervisor had closed all checkpoints but one and placed his entire staff there. The move would definitely slow traffic but it also meant the concentration of officers would increase the level of scrutiny. Then at 4:15, the supervisor began interviewing each duty officer to review whom they'd passed through since the shift began. Larkin was first.

Of the three cars she had waved through, the first one became an immediate candidate in her review because the driver was alone in the car. He was Caucasian and did not offer a passport. On the other hand, the latter bit was not unusual because he was a Canadian citizen and this type of border crosser frequently offered a driver's license with a photograph. The license, Larkin recalled, was from the province of Quebec and she had taken particular note of his face to match it with the photograph.

When she was asked about a possible mustache, Larkin was certain he did not have one but then strained her memory to recall whether it might have been recently shaved off. Finally, she concluded that even if it had been recently removed, the man's complexion was really too pale to tell. As for the hands, she had not seen them well enough to notice anything. The car, she explained, was a reasonably new Japanese model, and at first she had been curious about a ski pole in the back seat. A strange item in August, and even stranger in that there was just one. However, the driver explained he'd been hiking in the White Mountains of New Hampshire for the past week, a claim reinforced by a backpack and two empty water bottles on the floor of the back seat.

The second car also seemed to offer a possible candidate as it had a man with a bushy mustache in the front passenger seat. Coincidentally, Larkin also remembered that he had dirty hands or, at least, hands that had been wiped with less than perfect results. However, the bushy mustache was more gray than dark and the woman driving the car had asked if there were washroom facilities. They had just changed a flat tire, the woman explained, and wanted to clean up. Larkin regretted not opening the trunk of this car; it would have been both easy and natural and, if nothing else, would quite likely have confirmed or disproved the flat tire story.

The two offered U.S. passports immediately upon driving up, a gesture that usually indicated experience in crossing borders, and gave their reason for travel as pleasure. They were en route to visit relatives in Sherbrooke, east of Montreal. Since both claimed their home to be a small town that Larkin knew was in the northwest corner of the state of Massachusetts, this was an appropriate border crossing, and she had waved them through despite a nagging curiosity about the difference in their appearance. The woman was far more neatly and carefully groomed than the man with her.

The lone driver of Larkin's third car had caught her attention at first because he was sweating so profusely. Sometimes that was a sign of extreme nervousness; yet the man's car was an older one and it could be the air conditioning did not work. Besides which, Larkin noted, she was sweating herself. The weather had been sunny and hot for the past week and today had been more of the same. Nevertheless, what made her pay extra attention in this case was the man's passport. He was a Lebanese citizen. Although she constantly steeled herself against prejudice, any passport from the Middle East or Far East made her take special notice.

This driver was perhaps in his thirties and had no mustache but Larkin had no memory at all of his hands. She thought they might have been delicate but that impression may have come from her observation of the man as being of slight build. He claimed to be driving from Burlington, Vermont, where he worked (he had a green card) and was going west to Detroit, Michigan. When Larkin questioned why he was going into Canada, he offered the quite reasonable explanation that Canada offered an east-west freeway that could get him to Detroit faster. The interstates in the U.S., especially in this part of the country, run mostly north and south, he had added, a reason that Larkin, like all customs officers at this crossing, heard frequently. Still she had been curious, if not quite suspicious, and opened the man's trunk. It had a single suitcase, a laptop and a set of golf clubs: nothing to merit delaying him further so she passed him through.

When her review was complete, the supervisor was satisfied that none of her three candidates provided any real reason for suspicion and Larkin returned to duty. It was not until her shift was finished at midnight that she had time to reflect on the earlier part of the day. That was when it struck her that one of the three border crossers had lied.

Which one of the three border crossers had lied to Larkin?

Solution on page 172

Homicide at 24 North Bleaker Street

<u>File #3347D Subject: Tondayo, Keith L., homicide</u>

Detective Inspector Mira Mirakawa
Transcript of interview with Mrs. Jolene Werner, 10:30 a.m., April 15, 2006

MIRAKAWA: This is Detective Inspector Mira Mirakawa, badge number 215TM, speaking with Mrs. Jo ...

WERNER: I'll tell you what I saw all right I ...

MIRAKAWA: Mrs. Werner, I have to put certain information on the tape first before I ask you questions.

WERNER: You just go ahead but I know what I saw. People think just because — my son, he wants to put me in a home — it's that wife of his, she ...

MIRAKAWA: Just a minute Mrs. Werner... Mirakawa with Mrs. Jolene, that's J-O-L-E-N-E Werner W-E-R-N-E-R, 10:30 a.m., April 15, 2006, at her residence, 29 North Bleaker Street. Now we'll talk, Mrs. Werner.

WERNER: Yes, that fellow at 24. I never did know his name but he was only there a year. The Wardells used to live there. Herb and Vera. I'm here 42 years next July 17. On my own since Walter's gone. We lived over on Samson with his parents for 11 years before that. Got married right after the war you know.

MIRAKAWA: Yes, Mrs. Werner. Now, did you see anyone around Mr. Tondayo's residence yesterday?

WERNER: He never had visitors. Seemed like he was never there neither. Went out a lot at night too. Late, I mean, 2 and 3 in the morning and sometimes not come back for a couple days or more. You know that's just awful him being killed like that.

MIRAKAWA: But he was home yesterday, wasn't he?

WERNER: Well he come home in the morning from wherever he was. At 9 I heard him drive in. *The Dinah Macklin Show* ...

MIRAKAWA: You heard him, you didn't see him?

WERNER: I saw him. That chair there by the TV? You can see right across.

MIRAKAWA: But did you see anyone yesterday?

WERNER: No, like I said, he never had visitors. 'Course there was that survey woman in the afternoon.

MIRAKAWA: Survey woman?

WERNER: You know, one of those busybodies that come around wanting to know what toothpaste you like. Had one of those boards. Clipboards, that's it. Never came in here though. I wouldn't have let her in anyway. Don't like that kind of prying.

MIRAKAWA: What time was that? Do you remember?

WERNER: Right before *Oprah* so it was 4 o'clock.

MIRAKAWA: Could you describe her?

WERNER: Well, I never got a good look at her face. I was on the porch when she came see, and soon as she got out of her car and I figured what she was up to, I went inside. Was going to watch *Oprah* anyway. She was average height I guess, taller than you but then you're pretty short aren't you? Her hair was to the shoulder, blonde it was. She wore slacks. Came in a car, I saw that. Blue, one of those little foreign things.

MIRAKAWA: Did she go to other houses too?

WERNER: I don't know that. Like I said I wasn't going to let her in so I went to the back of the house. I got another TV there. Wanted it to look like I'd gone out.

End of transcript.

File #3347D Subject: Tondayo, Keith L., homicide

Detective Inspector Mira Mirakawa
Transcript of interview with Ms. Faith Orenda, 1 p.m., April 16, 2006

MIRAKAWA: Detective Inspector Mira Mirakawa with Ms. Faith F-A-I-T-H Orenda O-R-E-N-D-A, April 16, 2006, 1 p.m., at police head-quarters. Thank you for coming in, Ms. Orenda.

ORENDA: Do I need a lawyer?

MIRAKAWA: So far this is just routine. You were the deceased's partner?

ORENDA: Business partner. And that's former too. Our partnership ended three months ago. Look, I'm sure you know all this already. Keith and I did software development. Specialized in photo enhancement. He was the techie, I ran the business end. We parted because — you must know this — he was cheating. Running another service on the side. And if you're planning to ask me about Keith having a finger in the drug trade, I don't know a thing about that. He could have been for all I know. Wouldn't surprise me. There's cocaine all over the photo business now.

MIRAKAWA: Who said anything about cocaine?

ORENDA: Well, nobody I guess, but that's what's all over now — cocaine.

MIRAKAWA: I see. Could you tell us what is your relationship with Martin Verdecchi?

ORENDA: What did I say? You know everything already. Martin and I formed a legal business partnership six weeks ago.

MIRAKAWA: The two of you have the same home address, 12 Newton Road over in Dufferin.

ORENDA: We live together. That a crime or something? And our studio and office are over the garage. Martin had a unit downtown but he had to give that up when Keith made a deal with him and didn't come through. Martin lost all his hardware in the deal.

MIRAKAWA: Do you know a Mrs. Jolene Werner?

ORENDA: Never heard of her.

MIRAKAWA: How often were you at Keith Tondayo's house on North Bleaker Street?

ORENDA: Not once. Not ever. Keith's not the type you ever wanted to mix business and pleasure with.

MIRAKAWA: Where were you yesterday, April 15, 2006, between the hours of 3 p.m. and 5 p.m.?

ORENDA: Look, I want a lawyer. You said this was routine. Anyway, I was at home, with Martin.

MIRAKAWA: Anybody else who can verify that?

ORENDA: We were enhancing film. With our equipment, that's done with doors and windows closed. Now isn't that convenient for you?

MIRAKAWA: Yesterday Mrs. Werner saw someone who matches your looks at 24 North Bleaker.

ORENDA: Well she didn't see me.

MIRAKAWA: Blonde hair. About your height and weight.

ORENDA: I'm 5'5" and 114 pounds. Have you got any idea how many women would fit that description? I bet a lawyer does.

MIRAKAWA: Blonde hair is pretty hard to confuse.

ORENDA: What does an old lady know from blonde hair? Ten percent of the women in the world are blonde. And what about Miss Clairol? You want blonde, you can have blonde. You want blonde hair exactly like mine, all it takes is a trip to the drug store.

MIRAKAWA: Ms. Orenda, what kind of car do you drive?

ORENDA: It's a Honda Civic. And it's Marina Blue as if you didn't already know. One of the best selling cars in the world. Go into any parking lot in this city and you'll see a dozen exactly like it. As a matter of fact why don't you go and do that. I'm finished answering questions anyway.

Subject refused to answer further questions.

In this pair of interviews there is a clue that should convince Detective Inspector Mirakawa to probe deeper. What is that clue?

Solution on page 173

4

In Pursuit of Deserters

Sub-Lieutenant Julian Mainbridge sat on the bottom rung of a homemade ladder that led to the loft above him and pondered his next move. In Julian's view, there were three issues to sort out. One was that the woman was lying. There was no doubt of that. Yet — and here was the second issue — who could blame her? Like the rest of the peasant farmers in this hilly countryside, she'd had enough of war and killing so how could he fault her for looking out for herself? The third issue was entirely separate but one of far longer standing: his commanding officer was an idiot. Of the many reasons that Julian had to be resentful of his current state, that one was first and foremost.

What made things worse is that he felt so helpless, so utterly unable to do anything. Here he was in the duchy of Swabia of all places, galloping around the German countryside looking for deserters from the British army. Where he needed to be, if his career was going to go anywhere, was hundreds of miles to the south in Spain or Portugal, doing his bit to give Napoleon what for. But the odds of getting back there now, he knew, ran from slim to none. All because of his commanding officer. All because of Jack Aston.

The proper title was *Lord* Jack Aston for he was the fourth son of the Duke of Somerset, although every man in the regiment from aide-de-camp on down thought of him as "Lord Jackass." Papa, the Duke, had bought son Jack his commission, not hard to bring off when there's wealth enough to outfit an entire regiment. Julian himself was hardly innocent of the practice for his father too had bought him a commission, but Julian's father was a wine merchant in Liverpool, and the best his influence and money could muster for his son was a bottom rank. Still, it was a commission and Julian knew that in this war with Napoleon and the French, the opportunity to rise by merit was his to grasp.

He'd almost had the opportunity too, Julian did, less than a year ago in what was now becoming known as the Peninsular War. The regiment had landed in Portugal too late to be part of Sir Arthur Wellesley's initial victories, but it was immediately attached to the 17th Light Dragoons, right at the front of the advance into Spain. Its very first task, however, had resulted in total disgrace, entirely the fault of Lord Jackass.

Like many other officers in the British High Command, His Lordship had no military experience or training, and to make up for it he emphasized spit and polish. Regimental officers were expected to be in parade dress at all times even while on field duty, for this was the surest way, Aston believed, to properly distinguish them from the rabble they commanded and to impress the civilian simpletons in the countryside. Failure to attend a formal event — and there were many — was invariably punished. And of course, to miss dinner in the officers' mess was considered a major offense. Julian had learned to live with these annoyances, albeit with some sacrifice. Of the two horses his father had provided him, only one was parade ground quality in appearance, so he had to be careful about which one he rode and when. And unlike Aston, whose personal tailor was permanently assigned to the command tent, Julian was secretly making do with just one uniform.

What tipped the cart for Julian was Aston's sheer incompetence in the field, which had shone like a beacon in that very first assignment in Spain. The 17th had been attached to a force led by General Sir John Moore, a personal friend of King George, and was specifically directed to guard the left flank. But after crossing the Spanish border, Lord Jack had allowed Moore and the main force to get way ahead while he held the regiment in camp so they could properly celebrate his birthday with a formal parade. With their flank open, the British force had been overwhelmed and Moore was killed. Even the commander-in-chief, Sir Arthur Wellesley, didn't have the power to fire the son of a duke but he could — and did — punish him. Lord Jack and his entire regiment, Julian Mainbridge reluctantly included, were sent north into Germany to keep an eye on Napoleon's ally, Maximilian I of Bavaria. There would be no glory here.

From his seat on the ladder, Julian had a view out the open barn door to the rolling green hills. Here and there a few cattle grazed placidly, not as many as there would have been in the fields in a time of peace, for the peasants hid most of their stock in the forest. If there were any deserters to be found, that's where they would be too: hiding in the forest. Still, Julian had been assigned the unpleasant task of hunting down deserters long enough to know that they usually came out of the forest at night to steal food from farms like this one. Very often they didn't even have to steal, for here in Swabia the British were the enemy and therefore a British deserter ... well, "whoever harms my enemy is my friend."

Julian stood up slowly and took a step forward to check on his horse. It was still there, tethered to the fence where the woman had brought it water in a wooden bucket, and an armful of hay. The gesture had touched Julian, but then this was not the first time that kind of thing had happened. On the other hand, the horse was not an enemy and the woman, after all, was a farmer; to feed a working animal was instinctive. He flexed his shoulders a few times before peering at the sky, and then walked stiffly over to the horse. A bit of sun was forcing through the cloud cover now, a welcome sign after three days of steady rain.

The horse was sniffing about for a few remaining wisps of hay, so Julian waited a minute before mounting. He could tell the woman was watching him through a crack in the door of her house and he waved to her in a friendly way. He still hadn't worked out whether he'd give her a bit of money. His Lordship, from his own very deep pockets — or more likely his father's — had worked out a system for rewarding people who provided information and, despite the language barrier, the woman had made it clear to Julian that over the past few days, deserters had been coming in from the forest at dusk to spend the night in the loft.

In the end, Julian chose to leave a few coins for her. He put them on the fence where the horse had stood. She had lied to him but what difference did that make? In her own way, she too had to put up with Lord Jackass just as Julian did.

How does Julian Mainbridge know that the woman lied to him?

Solution on page 173

5

Count to Five, Press the Button and Get Out!

"Lumpy" Pechnik was concentrating so hard he didn't realize he'd chosen the women's lingerie department to hide in. Not that realizing it would have made any difference. There was no way he was going to screw this up — it was the easiest 500 bucks he'd ever scored. In fact, except for the time he'd scooped the cash from a gas station where the night attendant had a do-or-die case of the trots, this would be the *only* time Lumpy had ever held $500 in his hands at once. And it was going to be so easy! All he had to do was press a button!

There were a couple of things that had bothered him, but only for a minute. Lumpy was not given to long periods of reflection. One was that the two suits who approached him this morning — big guys they were too — how come they knew he could get into this big Sears store after hours pretty well whenever he wanted? And how come they knew his real name: Lamont? Nobody on the streets knew that. Why, nobody had called him Lamont since Sister Mary Magdalene had kicked him out of St. Anselm's. Well, no matter. All Lumpy cared about was that he was going to get big bucks for an easy touch.

What he had to do was keep an eye on the up escalator here on the first floor. When the security guard appeared, he was to count to five slowly — the suits were really emphatic about that part. They made him practice three or four times: "One steamboat, two steamboats..." like that. Then what he had to do was press the red button on this gizmo they'd given him and after that get out of the store. A couple streets over, on Sackville, he was to drop the gizmo down the sewer and then pick up his money at the 7-11: the *rest* of his money. Lumpy fingered the 50 bucks in his left shirt pocket. The suits were only going to give him 20 as a down payment and they didn't even want to give him that. Said he'd probably buy some Sneaky Pete wine and buzz out in an alley somewhere, but Lumpy held out for more and they'd sawed off at 50.

From his vantage point in women's lingerie, Lumpy could eyeball about half the first floor of the big Sears store. Even in the dimmed down, after-hours lighting he could make out just about everything for he had good eyesight. Despite the semi-darkness he was able to read prices a couple aisles away. He could even read the sign over the bottom of the escalator he was watching so carefully: "Women and Men's Clothing — Sporting Goods." Stuff like that. Way across the store he could pick out a broken 'E' in an exit light. Lumpy was proud of his sharp eyes. A lot of other guys on the street had been blitzed for so long their vision was shot, but not him.

He fingered the 50 bucks again. The security guard — the guy had to be showing up soon — what the suits had told him was that this guard always did his rounds at the same time, but Lumpy already knew that. He was a regular here at Sears. On really cold winter nights when he knew the temperature was going to drop out of sight, he would crawl into the building through an old drainage pipe and hide in a garbage bin in the sub-basement. Security only came to the sub-basement once a night. Up here on the first floor he was in strange territory, but that didn't threaten him.

What actually did bother him was the silence. Lumpy was used to noise. There was always noise on the street. The soup kitchens were noisy too. Even the sub-basement was noisy with the hum of the big heating units and the subway on the other side of the wall and the loading dock just down the passageway. On the other hand, it was the silence that enabled Lumpy to hear the approach of the guard a few seconds before he saw him. The suits were right about that part.

"The guard comes directly from the jewelry department to the up escalator," they had said. "They're not running after closing time, the escalators, so you should be able to hear him walking on it before you see him. The instant you see him on that escalator you count the way we practiced and on 'five steamboats' you hit the button and then get out of there!"

Lumpy put a flat, grimy thumb on the red button and the instant he saw an arm in a uniformed sleeve he began the count. On "five steamboats" he pressed down. Seconds later, when the guard disappeared from view, Lumpy slowly backed out of the lingerie department and easily found his way to the sub-basement. Next stop: the sewer over on Sackville and then into the 7-11 for his money. Duck soup. Easiest 500 bucks he'd ever made.

Did Lumpy earn his money?

Solution on page 173

The Case of the Open Safe

Stop me if I told you this already. The news on the TV made me think of it. They always got that TV going in the lounge downstairs but the only thing I ever watch is the news. You happen to see it this morning? About some no-good who says the door to a safe was wide open before he got there? No matter. It was only a couple of seconds on the TV and you likely missed it. See, it was just like the heist at Barney Rawn's Feed Store some ... some ... gotta be near 25 years ago now, I guess. Maybe 26 even. No matter. It was the year I retired from the force. That robbery, the one at Barney's I mean, the guy what did it was one of the last no-goods I collared.

Name was ... name was ... Y'know, it's just awful how I forget names now. I can see the faces, but do you think I can put a name to... *Lassiter!* That's the guy's name! Lassiter! Cleaned out old Barney's safe and then pretended he was the one discovered the cash was gone! Lotta nerve, eh? Come to think of it, he must be out by now, Lassiter. Got 20 years he did. See, he was on parole at the time, so the judge stuck him a good one. These guys never learn do they? Yea, he'd be out by now ... unless maybe he's dead; he was no young kid at the time. Old Barney, gosh, he's been gone now, I don't know how long already.

What's that? Oh, yeah, Lassiter and the safe. Well, you see it was like this. Barney Rawn's store was over on the east side of Langdon. You know where I mean: the street that runs straight south from the river. Car dealership there now, last I heard. Anyway, Barney's store ... pretty good size building it was ... single story with an alley along the south side. There was a kinda rundown warehouse the other side of the alley that belonged to Barney too. He kept feed on the main floor in that one and mostly junk up on the second.

What this Lassiter did ... did I mention he worked at the store? Barney, he was always takin' in bums, givin' 'em a job. Had a good heart, Barney, but it cost him. If I told him once, I told 'im a thousand times ... No matter. Anyway, Barney had a safe in this little storeroom at the back of the store. Kept it in a corner where the back wall meets the alley wall. That way it was pretty much outa sight of his customers 'cause the doorway was kitty corner. You know, like, on the diagonal. But there was no door in it. Too much bother, I guess, to open and close all the time. 'Specially if you're carryin' stuff.

Now, what this Lassiter did, from time to time he'd get himself over to the upper floor of the warehouse across the alley and watch Barney through the windows when he opened the safe. See, Barney had to really take his time 'cause his eyes were goin' so it didn't take much just to watch and figure out the combination. And then Lassiter always got to see everything that was *in* the safe too, 'cause old Barney, soon as he spun the combination, he'd open the door wide. Meant Lassiter could pick the best time to rob it. Clever enough, I guess.

Now, I know what you might be thinkin' but this ain't how I collared the guy. He — Lassiter, I mean — he told me all this about the combination and stuff after I arrested him, once he knew he was snookered anyway. No, how I caught him, or maybe it's better to put it this way: *how he snookered himself* was ... well, like this. He gets himself into the storeroom one night. Wasn't hard — Barney's place was like a sieve. To give this Lassiter credit though, we never did figure out and he never told us, how he got outa the halfway house. Lockdown there was always sunset and for sure he was out after midnight. Anyway, here's what he did.

Like I said, he gets himself into the storeroom, opens the safe and takes out the cash drawer. Next morning, he shows up at the front door for work. See, Barney always opened up and whoever worked for him had to be there at the door whenever Barney said. Usually it was 8 o'clock. So Barney opens the door and they go in and Lassiter, he goes right to the back to the storeroom but kinda casual-like. Makes sure that Barney sees that he doesn't go *in*. And then he yells from the doorway that the safe is open and the cash drawer is gone!

See, the way I figured, he knew he'd be a suspect for sure, him bein' on parole, so what he did was leave the safe door open so he could sorta announce what happened. I imagine he figured that would put him a step or two away from things. But do you know what he did wrong? How he trapped himself?

You *do*, don't you! I can see it in your face! Are you sure I haven't told you this before? Sometimes I forget, you know.

 What did Lassiter do wrong?

Solution on page 174

7

Getting to the Front Door

"That's the only way in. Through the gate there."

"You sure? The wall's not all that high."

"Yea, but they got motion sensor beams all along the top. Random too so y'never know just where they are. Can't go under. Over neither for that matter. Gotta go through the gate."

"Yet there's no live security on the gate. How come?"

"Right now it's seven — what — seven-twenty. They're live on the gate during the day. Just one guy but he's off at six. Unless they got a party on at the house or something like that. Then they leave the gate open but there's guards out here then. Otherwise on regular nights the guards patrol. Do rounds. Two of 'em — guards I mean — but they never change their round times so that'll be easy."

"What about a gate at the back? People with this kind of money don't want stuff coming in the front."

"No good. There's two of 'em — gates I mean — but both are manual and they're shut down at six."

"And you can't interrupt the perimeter system, the motion sensor?"

"Wireless. Main control's in the house."

"Okay, so first entry is through the gate here. I assume the keypad is under the flap on the left there?"

"No, above it. In that little hole at the end of the wall."

"It's called a *niche*. Why up so high?"

"Kids. So they can't reach it and fool around. The others are up just as high."

"Others. More than one keypad?"

"There's three."

"There *are* three. Two in addition to this one, I assume?"

"Yea. Pull ahead a bit and y'can see the next one closer to the house."

"There's a hydrant just ahead. Why do you think I parked here?"

"We're gonna heist a couple million bucks in diamonds and you're afraid of a parking ticket?"

"Use your head! We don't need the *attention*! Besides, I don't need to see the — ooh! Dobermans! Two — no, three of them!"

"I was going to get to that."

"My God, they're big! I suppose they run loose on the grounds until morning too. That could be a complication."

"Not on a warm night. Not for me anyway. They're somethin' else, those dogs. I mean, talk about training. They don't bark!"

"Probably had their larynxes surgically removed. I've heard of that."

"No, no, nothin' like that! They're really trained not to bark. It's for the neighbors, the noise thing. And they don't bite neither!"

"*Either*. And next you're going to tell me they play chess in their down time."

"No, no! They grab onto your clothes and hold on till the handler comes. Like, one of the guards."

"What then? They sign a release?"

"You don't get it! They bite somebody it's a big hassle for the owners. Some swell over on another street — he got sued big time."

"Well, if nothing else you appear to have integrated yourself into the neighborhood effectively. At least into the gossip."

"Hey, nobody sees me no more. Like you said, become like part of the whatsit."

"Vegetation."

"Yea, part of the vegetation. Worked too. That's how I got the code for the keypads."

"Keypad*s*? All three?"

"Yea. Talk about dumb. These people, they put in all this high price security and they got guards full time ... "

"And dogs that play chess ... "

"Whatever. And then they code all the pads the same! So's nobody's got to remember three different codes!"

"And you're sure you have the codes, or rather, the code, singular?"

"No sweat. Like, that keypad you don't want to see — your parking ticket keypad — it's closer to the house on this side of the fancy landscaping. That's where we spend most of our time, by the way, workin' on that part. They got more cedar than Yellowstone in there. Anyways, this pad controls the security around the house itself. More motion sensors, broken window detectors, that kinda stuff. Wireless like on the wall."

"That's not what I asked. *Do you have the code?*"

"One number to go. Well, really, one number to be *sure*. It's a five or a six. I just gotta watch the crew chief punch it one more time and like I said, it's no sweat. I can almost stand right beside him now when he puts it in. Part of the ve ... vegetation."

"The third keypad ... it must be at the main door. You sure it has the same code as the others?"

"Well ... yea, I see where you're comin' from. They don't exactly invite us into the house for tea but I seen one of the inside staff use it just yesterday, and it's the same."

"It better be, or the whole operation stops at the door."

"There's, uh, one thing. Don't mind me askin' but they gotta have big time security inside. How're you gonna ...?"

"Not your concern. Your job is to get us to the front door."

"Count on it. I suppose you wanna wait for a warm night?"

"Naturally."

 Why do the jewel thieves want to wait for a warm night?

Solution on page 174

8

Leave No Trace

Moira Catesby put the Gucci tote bag by the front door and turned to go back through the apartment one more time. Finding a pair of her panty hose in the closet of the spare bedroom had given her a start and she was worried she might have missed something else.

The spare bedroom was her first stop on this second go round, particularly the closet, for that's where she'd kept a few clothes for the occasional times she stayed over. This time she was confident that nothing was left behind. The same was true for the master bedroom. Even so she lay down on the floor one more time and, with a penlight, checked that nothing of hers had fallen under the bed over the past several months and been forgotten. The bathroom, kitchen and bar were next, but before covering them she took a last, critical look at Jacques Ste-Lowe lying in the bed, noting that even in death he looked organized and in control, as if this thing was all his idea.

Moira had shot Jacques behind the left ear as he got into bed and he'd folded quietly into a dignified shape with arms and legs together. Most victims shot that way would stiffen in shock or thrash about before spreading into a contorted form. Moira knew that better than most because she killed people for a living. But for Jacques there was no indignity and no uncontrolled reaction. She could almost imagine him setting out the appropriate suit for the funeral and making his precious lists: a list of mourners, a list of appropriate flowers, a list of dates and times and responsibilities for the funeral ceremony. For a brief second, Moira was tempted to ruffle his hair or do something to disrupt the apparent serenity. But only for a second. She owed him that much.

In the kitchen and at the living room bar she wiped every bottle and glass one more time. Even a partial fingerprint could be a threat. The bathroom got a rigorous second check. There was no way she was going to leave makeup or a toothbrush, much less some potential for DNA like a toothpaste spatter. That's why she was even taking the kitchen garbage with her, although she was positive there was nothing in it that would lead to her. Still, she knew it always paid to be over-cautious. That was why she had put new sheets on Jacques' bed before she'd shot him but had been careful not to get into the bed herself.

Moira returned to the front door and picked up the Gucci bag, then set it down and made one last check of the living room. It occurred to her she hadn't looked behind the drapes in her first inspection. This time she was satisfied. She picked up the bag, peeked through the security hole in the door to be sure the hall was empty, and then walked out to the stairs. Nobody in the building ever used the stairs except the cleaning staff and, at 11 p.m., it was a safe bet there were none of them around. A doorman would be on duty in the lobby but Moira had always come in through the underground garage.

She reached her car without encountering anyone, popped the locks and got in. She put her key in the ignition but then changed her mind and sat back. Better to wait a second or two, she thought, and catch her breath, for the adrenaline was pumping hard. Not because she was frightened or physically stressed but because just for a moment — only a moment — she'd had a twinge of regret. Jacques had been, well … Jacques had been an okay guy. Mind you, Jacques Ste-Lowe probably wasn't his real name. Hers wasn't Moira Catesby either; it was Beth Shlomo, but still …

Actually the assignment had gone like clockwork. She'd worked herself into Jacques' life over the past several months, but not too closely. Not moving in with him full time or anything like that, just tight enough to be important in his life without becoming part of it. That way she didn't have to meet other people he knew and that was always an open door for the cops. No, the relationship had worked at just the right frequency: the odd dinner date like the one earlier tonight but never more than once every week or two. They went to an occasional show, just the two of them — both of them were big fans of musicals. And from time to time in nice weather they would walk in the park, but that was as far as she'd allowed things to develop.

Moira sighed and started the car and then looked into the Gucci bag, taking inventory almost subconsciously. The Smith & Wesson .22 with the silencer: that would go into the Don River when she crossed the Bloor viaduct. The makeup kit too. No good to use a dumpster these days the way the homeless crawled around in them. With sudden intensity, she reached into the bag — *where were those confounded panty hose?* — and then felt relief. They were there, along with the dress she'd worn last week, an extra skirt and sweater, a negligee, and — she counted them twice — the exact number of items of underwear. Everything was there except for — where was it? — ah, there: Jacques' cell phone. She never called Jacques on his apartment line, only on his cell and only from her cell. These, too, would go into the Don with the gun and the makeup. It was important that she leave no trace of herself at all.

If Moira wishes to leave no trace of herself, there should be one more item in the tote bag. What is that?

Solution on page 174

9

A Great Future in Art Forgery

"You were not exaggerating. This kid's a genius!"

"What did I tell you? I bet Gainsborough himself would say this is one of his. Of course we'll have to age it. All the usual. Put it in a distressed frame. Like that."

"But he's got it down so *absolutely!*" Blaine Talley shook his head in admiration and disbelief as he raised himself from a stooping position. He winced as he arched his back and drew both arms backward as far he could, elbows bent. The painting he'd been examining so carefully stood on a low easel and Blaine was an exceptionally tall man.

"What's his name?" Blaine wanted to know.

"Jean-Luc Benoit."

"So he's French."

"He's from Quebec. You'll have to let him tell you whether that means he's French."

Blaine muttered a mild "Hmmpf" and bent over the painting once more, a large magnifying glass in his hand. The work was an oil on canvas, a portrait of a young teenage boy dressed in the ultimate fashion of late 18th-century Europe. Except for the white knee-length stockings and the dark hat, all the clothes were blue.

"What I don't get," Blaine was talking to himself as much as to the man who'd invited him into the studio, "what I don't get is why he'd put this much work into a *joke*! Not all that good a joke either."

The subject of the portrait, whom Blaine and his host were already calling "Blue Boy," was sitting on the ground, resting against a fallen log in an idealized English countryside. In the background, rough hills rose to a sky that offered an exciting combination of threatening clouds, backlit by sunshine that did not quite break through.

"It's not a joke, Blaine! You said yourself the kid has Gainsborough down cold. Look at the blue on that prissy suit. I mean, it actually floats!"

Blaine had to agree. Jean-Luc Benoit had captured perfectly the velvet sheen on the clothes the boy was wearing. The shading made it look like he'd only just sat down.

"And look at the — the whaddaya call — accessories? The hat, the glove, the cane."

On the ground to the boy's immediate left, just barely touching his knee, lay an overlarge hat with a fluffy white plume that soared out of the brim and then tumbled over his leg. On the other side of the hat lay a glove of matching white, palm up, the thumb under the brim and the fingers limp.

Blaine straightened up again, with a grimace all too familiar to anyone with back problems. "He's got the hat right," he said, "but Gainsborough's blue boy doesn't wear gloves. And he doesn't have a cane either!"

On the boy's left, resting at an angle slightly off perpendicular, lay a cane almost as long as the boy was tall. Its head almost covered the other glove, but delicately and not quite completely so that on one side the thumb could be seen gently brushing the boy's elbow. On the other, there was just a touch of the glove's embroidery visible in a soft red pattern.

"Of course Gainsborough's boy doesn't have a cane. Or gloves. And before you say it, Blaine, in *The Blue Boy*, the kid's shoes are light beige and they've got those little girl ribbons tied in a bow. Jean-Luc's blue boy here has dark brown shoes with buckles. And as for the position, the whole world knows blue boy is *standing*. But so what! That's not the point. I mean, the *point* is that... "

"I've got to admit, your man Jean-Luc," the French pronunciation rolled easily off Blaine's tongue, "he's got the atmosphere just dead on here. A teenage boy bored out of his wits. Family's got more money than God. And he's got to sit for a portrait."

"That's what I'm saying! That's how good this kid Benoit is. I mean, look at that sky! I bet he could do Constable and Turner too. See, that's my point! Look at those light brush strokes. Is that Gainsborough or what? Think of it! Who's to say that this *isn't* a real Gainsborough. A fascinating new discovery! Can't you see the headlines? Not to mention the check? I mean, we all know Gainsborough did portraits because he had to. It was income. He'd much rather have done landscapes."

Blaine was nodding, but it was not possible to tell whether he was agreeing with the biographical truth about Thomas Gainsborough or with the obvious proposal he was about to hear.

"Who's to say Gainsborough didn't do this one as a test run before the one we all know? You can see for yourself. There's everything in here! It's definitely the same kid. He's just sitting instead of standing. Background's not all that different from *Blue Boy*. The color's right. He's got that all-grown-up look they gave kids in the 18th century. I mean, what's not to like? Even if we don't market this one, you can see Benoit's got a future if we handle him right.

"What's he do when he's not reproducing masters?" Blaine wanted to know.

"Uh, well, uh, right now he drives a bus."

"A bus driver!" For the first time in several minutes, Blaine stopped rubbing the small of his back. "A *bus* driver." His guffaws echoed around the room.

"What's so funny about that? The guy's got to eat. At least until we get him set up and start peddling his stuff."

"Okay, okay, Sully. It's just that — well, I don't know very many bus drivers, and I certainly don't know any with a sense of humor like this. Look, I agree. He's got an enormous talent, but we're going to have to control it. Especially if he's into pulling off jokes like this one. At least, I *hope* it's a joke and not a dumb mistake!"

 Blaine has detected a flaw in the painting that is either a joke or an error. What is the flaw?

Solution on page 174

10

A Rush Order

Edna Pennycastle couldn't really remember the last time she'd been angry. It just wasn't in her nature. Sure, there was the time about a year ago when she had been looking over her parole supervisor's shoulder and saw him write "phlegmatic" on her behavior chart and that had come close to annoying her until he explained what it meant. And once in a while certain members of her social circle would test her patience by trying to avoid paying for a round of beers when it was definitely their turn. But for the most part, Edna's style was one of steady, unruffled calm. Until today. Today she had become very close to being downright indignant.

It all started innocently enough when Edna sauntered into the Romney Ram on Tooley Street about 10 a.m., as she often did. The Romney was her favorite pub in the Mechanics Bay area of Auckland, only a short walk from the fancy restaurants just to the west where she did her best work. And the publican didn't mind serving his regulars in the back room before or after hours. Edna was just beginning to sip a pint of Steinlager when Hilly Cranston came through the door in his typically noisy fashion. He was obviously in a rush and obviously looking for her. He needed a passport, Hilly told her, for one of his special people and it didn't matter from what country.

When Edna wanted to know why he didn't just go ask "Eversharp" McCreedy like everyone else did, Hilly replied that Eversharp, good as he was, took too long to produce the goods and this passport was needed by 4 p.m. After that, Edna just stared at her Steinlager and didn't say another word while Hilly fumed and fussed and kept raising the fee until his final offer topped out at $2000, upon which she nodded quietly and smiled. Edna had always found that her most effective negotiating strategy was complete silence.

After pocketing half the fee and accepting a promise of the remaining half on delivery, Edna found herself back out on Tooley Street debating whether to walk or take a taxi. Although she had never lifted a passport before, not that she could remember anyway, picking a pocket for one wouldn't be all that different from seeking out the usual fare. The only problem was where to find the clientele. However, that issue was quickly resolved when she remembered a time a few years ago when she had followed some poufy swell who'd been flashing a big bankroll and relieved him of it over on Ponsonby Street in front of a passport office. What could be a more logical place to steal a passport!

This was the point, though, when her change in mood began. The taxi dropped her off at the passport office — she'd chosen the softer option to save time — and to her surprise and extreme annoyance she discovered the front entrance was manned by a pair of security guards who were not only issuing numbers to people wanting in, but were asking for identification of all things! *And* they were dutifully recording this information in a laptop computer! Edna had never seen the like! Such a monumental waste of taxpayer's money! Not that Edna paid taxes herself — the less the government knew the better. But what a *waste!*

With indignation swelling, Edna turned away and walked down Ponsonby. Of all the ridiculous ... Who would have thought ... Most irritating of all: what to do now? She was going to have to give back ... But before that thought reached its disappointing conclusion, the sound of a large passenger jet overhead intruded. Of course! Where else do you find passports besides the passport office? At the airport!

The relief at having an alternate resource should have diluted Edna's irritation, but calculating that it would cost her about $30 just to get out to Auckland's airport and 30 more to come back stirred it up anew. It didn't help either that she went to the domestic terminal first and spent an hour wandering around grumbling to herself until she realized that it was the international one she wanted. Correcting that mistake too took time and more cash.

Still, Edna discovered, it's a truly ill wind that fails to blow at least a little bit of good, for in the process of getting herself to the international terminal she happened upon a trash barrel full of brochures of just the right color. She picked one out, folded it to size and moved along. By now, her strategy was pretty well formed and within minutes she found herself on the arrivals level in the middle of an atmosphere that went a very long way toward making her feel better. Arrivals was extremely busy. Perfect conditions.

With her righteous umbrage fading now to a mild burn, Edna shifted into professional mode. After first casually scoping out and noting anyone wearing a uniform, she picked her subjects: a large tour group clustered near a currency exchange. Almost unnoticed, she walked into their midst with the folded brochure barely visible in one hand.

"Anybody drop their passport?" she asked.

What does Edna expect her strategy to achieve?

Solution on page 175

11

Undercover with the Black Lasers

Quite likely it was the very ordinary task of brushing his teeth, but whether or not that simple act was the cause, George Trask broke a cardinal rule of undercover work that morning: he allowed himself to reflect on the danger of his situation. Bent over the sink in the not very clean clubhouse bathroom, while water gushed from the tap, George had let himself stare at the little white curl of paste on the toothbrush and admit to himself that he might never come out of this alive.

"You never, *never* let yourself stop to think about the risk." He could actually hear the gravelly voice of his instructor warning him, "for the simple reason that it's in front of you all the time. When you're undercover," the instructor went on, "it's all about danger and if you let yourself think consciously about that, two things will happen, the two *worst* possible things: you'll stop acting naturally *and* you'll lose your nerve, your edge."

As he stared into the spattered mirror George could also hear his own voice: something he'd said to his contact in their only meeting since the assignment began.

"These are really bad guys," he'd reported, as if the Bureau didn't already know that. "I've worked biker gangs back home, but this bunch ... there's nothing they won't do to protect their operation. And they don't wait for solid proof either!"

The Bureau man just nodded while George continued. "That floater, the guy you fished out of the bay on Memorial Day? You know, don't you, that it was the Lasers took him down?"

The Bureau man nodded again.

"Well, at the club they had a *competition* to see who got to do it!" Recalling the gruesome details of that murder made George shudder and brought him back to the present so that he stopped staring at his toothbrush and instead began to use it. Other Lasers would soon be up and about and wanting into the bathroom.

George Trask had been a probationary member of the Black Lasers Riding Club now since January. Despite the extremely high level of suspicion and distrust in the group, his insertion had actually been fairly easy. One reason was that the ATF, the Bureau of Alcohol, Tobacco and Firearms, had penetrated the Lasers some time before so there was a back door already open. The other was that George could speak Hebrew and the club desperately needed that skill. The Black Lasers were in the business of importing illegal weapons from Israel.

In reality, George was a Mountie, on loan from the Canadian force to the ATF. He'd grown up in Winnipeg where a Jewish community had thrived for years, and until his 25th birthday had visited Israel regularly. To the Lasers, he was a country boy from rural Saskatchewan, on the lam from Canadian authorities after they'd discovered a huge marijuana grow-op on his farm.

George rinsed his toothbrush and straightened to get a better look in the mirror. Satisfied that everything appeared to be as it should, he made a quick swipe with his underarm deodorant, grabbed his shaving kit, turned off the tap and opened the door only to run into Arnie "the Ferret" Garwich.

"For a while there I thought you were camping out!" Arnie grinned as he spoke, but there was no humor in his eyes. Arnie didn't have humor. He wasn't burdened by morality either, or by compunction of any kind, so that night, when the Lasers' executive voted to eliminate George, they knew Arnie was the right man to do it. Besides, it was Arnie who first brought it to their attention that their new Hebrew-speaking negotiator was likely not what he pretended to be.

 What led Arnie to suspect George?

Solution on page 175

12

Deadly Treasure Hunt

At low tide, a broad, white sand beach stretched to the east as far as the eye could see. The same was true on the westward shoreline, but in the distance the soft white line came to a sudden stop against a giant cliff. Rolling inland to the north, grassy dunes led the way toward higher ground and dense forest. Then, almost at the horizon, the slope curved sharply upward into a mountain range, an elevated spine that divided the island in half. The mountains were covered in mist on this particular morning; it was the dry season, but the men on the beach knew they were there all right. They'd seen the peaks during their struggle through the pounding surf.

The men had come in at high tide, six of them in a battered wooden dory. Two were dead now. They lay side by side in a pool of blood that was slowly soaking into the sand. Their hands were tied behind their backs and their throats were cut.

Of the remaining four men, three stood in a close knot. From a distance it looked like they might be quarrelling, but in fact they were having an animated debate over what looked like a ragged handkerchief and had to stand close together to be heard. Whatever they

were discussing involved the fourth man, for there was much pointing at him and from time to time all three would pause and look as
if they were waiting for him to contribute. This fourth man was sitting on the sand, knees up, with a large stick protruding from
beneath his knees on either side. His upper torso was pulled forward
because his arms were under the stick with his hands in front of his
knees. A long strip of canvas had been wound around the wrists,
binding them tightly. Blood oozed from the man's nose and both
sides of his face were bruised.

The three debaters were dressed haphazardly in rough clothing,
much of it made of the canvas that bound the fourth man. Two of
them, however, in odd contrast, wore black knee-length boots. The
third had wooden shoes. This man was further distinguished by a
blue coat that was too big for him. The source of these unusual addi-
tions was obvious for one of the two dead men wore remnants of a
uniform; the other had been stripped naked. The man with his wrists
tied wore a white shirt, brown woolen breeches and white knee
stockings, and he was the only man on the beach with leather shoes.
This man was named Culver and the reason he was still alive was that
he was a merchant who could read and write and do sums; the two
dead men could not. Nor could the three killers. Whether Culver
would live or die in the next minutes or hours or even days turned
on his ability to use those skills. They were needed to interpret the
letters and numbers on the handkerchief.

The handkerchief was made of the ubiquitous canvas that already
played so many roles in this scene, but that was not the reason for
its value. The handkerchief was a map, of that much the three men
were certain. That it was a map leading to buried wealth was something on which they could only speculate, but they were confident
enough in its promise to have murdered two men already. For them,
the next issue was singular: could they force Culver to read the map

without killing him or harming him so badly he could not — or would not — do the job? For Culver, on the other hand, there were two issues. One was obvious: how to drag this out as long as possible in the hope of eventual rescue or escape. The other was, could he actually read the map? It was a kind of code, a puzzle, and he knew if he could uncover its secret, he might just be able to manipulate his captors more effectively.

While the three debaters had been brutally uncovering the fact that his fellow captives were completely baffled by the map — if it could be called that — Culver had had a good look at it. The information on it had been written with charcoal or some kind of unreliable ink, for one bit of it had been smudged. That smudge caused him considerable uneasiness because it obliterated a key piece of information, almost certainly a numeral. The letter beside the smudge was still clear: an *M*, which Culver was sure stood for 'miles.' That abbreviation alone, if he survived till it came up, would give him extra time for, being seamen, his captors would definitely take it as 'nautical miles.' Culver was betting they wouldn't know these are longer than miles on land, until he made himself yet more indispensable by informing them.

Beside the *M* were more letters: *NNW*, and some numbers: *331*. Having noted similar coding elsewhere on the map, Culver believed these letters and numbers simply meant 331 degrees north-north-west by compass. But whatever was lost to that smudge had to be the *number* of miles!

The other batches of numerals and letters elsewhere on the map were clear. In a column from the top of the map, they read *77R-NNE18*. Culver had realized almost immediately that this meant 'go 77 rods north-northeast at 18 degrees.' Below that was *49Y-ESE110*. Then came *36C-E90* and *18F-SSE165* and finally, the problem one: smudge *M-NNW331*. Culver knew the numerals were a sequence of some kind; they had to be. But what sequence? Not knowing frustrated him enormously as he'd figured everything else out. At *36*, the *C-E90* had to mean 'go due east at 90 degrees for a distance of 36 chains.' (That *C* was another opportunity to gain time for Culver felt he could confuse the three with *C* possibly meaning 'cubit' instead of 'chain.' And the *F* at *18* might mean either 'furlong' or 'fathom.')

But it still came down to the smudge. What number had been written there?

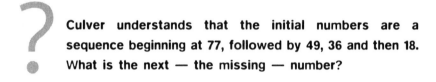

Culver understands that the initial numbers are a sequence beginning at 77, followed by 49, 36 and then 18. What is the next — the missing — number?

Solution on page 175

13

Too Much Medication?

Marissa Brezlaw was lying face down, legs stretched out behind her, as she strained to push her head and left arm under the old lady's bed. In that awkward position she didn't hear anyone come into the room. The voice, however, was familiar — and annoying.

"What's the matter, drop a quarter?"

Marissa's first instinct was to reply with an even better smart crack. Her second was to put on a moral superiority hat and say something about the crudity of making jokes at the bedside of a corpse. She did neither. Instead Marissa continued to wriggle farther under the bed until she got her fingers around an empty pill bottle.

"Must be a whole dollar," the voice added. "You're really trying."

Once again, Marissa successfully swallowed the words on the edge of her tongue but embarrassed herself nevertheless by tangling one foot in the old lady's walker and knocking it over as she rolled to get out from under the bed. In the same movement she bumped her head on the bed rail and then, to compound things, inhaled a dust bunny so that the first thing she did when she stood up was heave out a mighty sneeze.

Freddy Lockeron held out a tissue. "They also serve who only stand and wait," he said.

"Milton." Marissa recognized the line but immediately regretted giving Freddy another opportunity.

"Yes, John Milton, from 'On His Blindness'."

She was going to say "1652" but not only was she unsure of the year Milton wrote his famous poem, she knew from experience that these little contests with Freddy were unwinnable. Instead she turned professional.

"Melformin," she said, wiping a thin trace of dust off the label on the pill bottle. "This is *you!*" she added, peering a little more closely. "So that's why you're here."

"Type 2 diabetes," Freddy said, responding to her professional approach. "I put her on about a year ago when it became obvious that diet control wasn't doing the job any more. She was 76 — er, 77 — so that makes her 78 now. The arthritis was getting pretty bad too, especially lately."

Marissa turned to look once more at the body on the bed. The old lady's white hair made an aura against the dark green pillow. She'd been dead long enough now so that the final stages of rigor mortis were passing and her thin body had relaxed so that underneath the duvet it was almost unnoticeable.

"How long has she been your patient?" Marissa asked.

"Since we — since I opened practice here. That's what — 15 years now?"

Marissa didn't miss the "we." She and Freddy had come to Carberville at the same time, both recent medical school graduates, both opening a first practice. They had made a few desultory attempts at dating in the first year and Freddy had got quite interested but Marissa never got past the first steps. After she'd made it clear the relationship was going nowhere they'd gone through a period of barely being civil to each other, not a productive situation in a town with only three doctors. It was Marissa who made the effort to turn the relationship into one of polite professionalism, in part, although she would only admit it to herself in her darkest moments, because she never ever came out on top in their frequent verbal face-offs.

"The melformin," Marissa put the bottle into her briefcase. "You increase the dosage recently?"

Freddy reddened. "I did exactly what you would do! And what anybody else would do! Different dosage levels over several months until it seemed right. And yes, she needed a step-up about a week ago. In fact, she was scheduled for blood work tomorrow."

"Freddy, I'm not ..."

"And *before* you ask, I'm perfectly aware of that kidney study about the possible dangers of melformin. And you know, and I *know* that you know, it's not conclusive and it hasn't been replicated. In fact ..."

"Freddy! Freddy!" Marissa held up her hands in a braking motion. She knew his sensitivity had deeper roots than questions about his choice of medication. Two years before, Carberville's long-time coroner had retired and, unbeknownst to each other, they had both applied for the job. Though she admitted it would have stung if Freddy had won over her, she also knew that she would eventually have grown past it. But she was the coroner now. Freddy never quite got over losing out and never would.

Marissa took a long, deep breath, forcing herself to appear more casual than she felt. "Freddy, I really doubt that the medication has anything to do with Mrs. Panadopolos's death. I really do. The autopsy will tell us yea or nay, but right now ..."

"You're going to do an autopsy?"

Once again, Marissa drew out an extended breath. "Yes," she replied. "I'll grant you that first consideration with an old lady who has diabetes would be that she simply died of natural causes. Maybe diabetic coma — after all, she's late 70s. And it's only ..."

"You're going to do an autopsy on an old lady, 78 years old, who's got diabetes and lives alone and dies in her bed?"

"The police are going to ask for one anyway, Freddy, so I'm not going to wait. You can see for yourself there's something very wrong with this whole scene."

"You're going to call the police in?"

"Yes."

"Because you think there's been a crime here?"

"Yes."

"Then shouldn't you have put gloves on to pick up the pill bottle? And put it in an evidence bag?"

It was Marissa's turn to redden. Freddy never missed a chance to score points.

Why does Marissa believe there is evidence of a crime here?

Solution on page 176

14

Detective Aylmer's Report

FROM THE DESK OF
R.A. VAN STEEBEN, COMMISSIONER OF POLICE

<u>Emmett</u> - Media are hammering us for Aylmer's slow response yesterday on the Blackburn shooting, especially KLM-TV. The vic died a few minutes ago in the O.R. Press conference noon today.
What have you got? I need it <u>now!</u>
                                    Richard

<u>Richard:</u> Aylmer's report attached. Explains the delay. Also shows hole in Blackburn's story! We now have confirmation Blackburn fired Mateo for cause August 3. Evidence <u>not yet confirmed</u> Mateo having affair with B's wife.
                                    Emmett

Investigator's Report:
investigator's weapon used *
investigator's weapon not used ___

Date: Sunday, August 13

Officer: Martin Aylmer, Detective Constable

Division: Major Crimes (MC)

10:55 a.m. En route on Talliser Drive West re File
#96274 (Capistani). Responded to all-call for near-
est MC officer - shooting at 8788 Talliser Dr W.

10:58 a.m. Diverted by road closure on Talliser.
South on Crowfoot Trail to Poundmaker Blvd, then
west to Kelsey St and back up to Talliser.

underlining above is mine.
                                    Emmett

11:14 a.m. Arr. Blackburn Building at 8788 Talliser
W. Main entrance at front of building locked.
Called for backup and accessed building through
rear shipping dock on north side. Arr. scene
(office of Dennis Blackburn) c.11:25 a.m.

11:25 a.m. - c.1:30 p.m. Action at scene
Office door open wide. Victim (later identified -
Juan Carlo Mateo) on floor just inside bleeding
from possible gunshot wound in chest. One other
person present (later identified - Dennis

Blackburn) standing at opposite side arms raised.
Called for ambulance after determining no other
individuals present. Summoned crime scene team.

*Richard – Ambulance was dispatched at 11:28.
Like Aylmer, was detoured by closure on
Talliser. Arr scene at 11:59. Em.*

Investigator's Notes

#1: Blackburn <u>immediately</u> admitted shooting Mateo
with handgun and pointed to gun on window ledge
approx. three paces distant. (Weapon an automatic –
awaiting information on make, caliber and registry.)
This officer held Blackburn at gunpoint in corner of
office until backup arrived, arrested him and read
rights.

#2: Suspect (Blackburn) gave following info <u>after</u>
being read rights <u>in presence of backup.</u>
That he believed he was being followed by disgruntled
former employee (the victim, Mateo) who has a history
of violence (not yet verified); that he (suspect) was
planning a golf game this day but detoured via his
office to put some valuables in the safe, which has
a handgun inside loaded and cocked. Suspect says he
was at open safe and looked up to see reflection of
victim in office windows, arm raised with large soap-
stone carving in his hand. Turned and fired the gun
in self defense. (At entry, carving could be seen on

floor near victim.) Suspect entered via shipping dock
rather than disable security system at main door and
believes victim entered that way too. Suspect admits
he is uncertain but believes he saw victim on street
minutes before the shooting. Office is on second
floor in the center of the building, right above main
entrance and offers good view of Talliser. Clear
sunny day with very little traffic.

Use of Weapon: Weapon drawn from point of entry to
Blackburn Building until backup arrived c.11:45 a.m.
Weapon not discharged. See verification DWR 7099-
08/13.

Martin Aylmer D.C., Major Crimes

What is the "hole" in Blackburn's story?

Solution on page 176

15

An Impulse Rewarded

Melody had been in the root cellar of the old farmhouse once before. That was back in May: the 28th to be precise, the day Jason Corby was reported missing. She had found the cellar a truly intriguing place, with its floor of hard-packed earth and walls of whitewashed stone, and a ceiling so low she had to bend at the waist. What had impressed Melody particularly about the root cellar was the coolness of the place, and the dampness, and the pungent odor of potatoes and carrots and turnips past their prime after a winter in storage. She was a city girl, and the cellar offered a sensory journey she'd never had before.

The pleasure of sorting out the smells, however, and the novelty of allowing the atmosphere to wash over her was short-lived. Melody was a cop and she was revisiting the cellar on business. That morning her sergeant had sent her to the Corby farm to take down the police department's yellow tape. The inquest was over now, and although the verdict was inconclusive, the department had done all it could do in the case of Jason Corby's death. All that remained now was to declare the case closed or move it to the cold files.

"Better do a walkthrough of the house while you're out there," the sergeant had added, "the barn and the outbuildings too. With nobody but us around the place for the past ... what, six, seven months? ... it's probably a good idea to check for break-ins or whatever. If Corby's two daughters ever settle the fight over his will ... You probably heard that one of them wants to move in and the other wants to sell? Anyway, let's be sure there's nothing more to add to the file."

During the walkthrough Melody was relieved to discover the entire property intact. No sign of a break-in, no evidence of vandalism, just the sad loneliness of a home suddenly left empty. Jason had lived alone since his second wife died several years before. Although he had rented the land to a neighbor to keep the farm productive, Jason had chosen to stay in the house where he had been born and raised, where five generations of Corbys had grown and thrived. Unfortunately, unless the matter of his will, or rather, *wills* was resolved, he might be the last.

Six months before, on the May 28th date that Melody remembered well, one of Jason's daughters had called the police to say she had not heard from her father in some time, that no one remembered seeing him and that she could not find him anywhere. Three days later, on June 1st, his body was found at the bottom of a steep ravine on a nearby farm. The precise time of death, and whether or not he had died accidentally, proved difficult to resolve. Because the body had lain undiscovered for some time, the best the medical examiner could offer was that Jason had been dead for a week or more before the body was discovered. Then at the inquest, the ME had told the jury that "a week" was his best, educated guess. The time of death, he said, although certainly not less than a week, could have been as much as nine or even ten days prior to the discovery of the body.

As for how he died, Jason's fishing tackle was found at the top of the ravine and one of his favorite fishing holes was a short distance away, so it was possible his skull had been fractured in a fall, for the ravine was deep and craggy. But both his arms were broken between the wrist and elbow, something the ME suggested might be defensive wounds.

Although the matter of Jason Corby's estate did not influence the inquest, his two daughters, his sole survivors, were now involved in a vicious tangle over what they claimed were separate, valid wills. One daughter was in possession of a will that was over twenty years old. It gave her possession of the farm. Her half-sister claimed to have found a far more recent will in her father's papers, a will with much different terms. It was dated May 21, only ten days before Corby's body was found. Both wills had been hand-written in a block letter form on which separate handwriting experts had already offered differing opinions, and neither will had been witnessed. Although the newer will was clearly suspicious — it was entirely possible that Jason Corby was already dead on May 21 — the older will was dated before the second daughter was born. It was a true lawyer's battle.

Melody's decision to leave the root cellar to the end of her walk-through had been quite deliberate. As she'd got out of the patrol car that morning she realized that the emptiness of the old farmhouse would fill her with sadness and that her fascination with the root cellar might relieve it. She never did quite determine just what it was that made her lift a plastic bag off a hook in the ceiling and look inside. It was simply an impulse. Had the bag been hanging there during her first visit? She had no idea. Maybe, maybe not. It was off to the side and could easily have gone unnoticed.

Her intent had been to open it and sniff, to see if there was yet another smell in the root cellar that she could experience. There were tulip bulbs in the bag, several dozen of them, and they indeed offered a new odor, especially when Melody put her face right into the bag. That was when she saw the note: just the edge of it as it was covered by a layer of bulbs. Simple curiosity made her reach in and take it out, for there was no reason to believe it had anything to do with Jason Corby's death, his will either. Except for the date. The note said — in clear block letters — "dug out & stored May 22 a.m." Melody stared at the note, as if her concentration would make the writing disappear or correct itself or... she didn't know what. She flicked the edge of the paper back and forth with one fingernail, blinked and then read the note again.

Very slowly and gently she set the note on the earthen floor and backed out of the cellar. Her next task was to go out to the patrol car for an evidence bag. This note was definitely going to stir up the fight over the wills.

Will Melody's discovery support the veracity of the newer will or the older one?

Solution on page 177

16

A Second Opinion on the Case

"Would you mind just taking a look?"

Ivor Noonam had been retired for just 18 months and already his wife, Vera, was convinced that "Would you mind just taking a look?" might be the phrase that would undermine their golden years. Ivor had been head of Scotland Yard's Criminal Investigation Division in Manchester for 11 years before he talked himself into accepting a pension, something he'd done so that he and Vera could "scratch a long-time itch, mostly his," as Vera put it. The itch was to own a small bed and breakfast in Coven, a tiny village in the Peaks District.

The B&B had turned out to be enormously successful, largely owing to Ivor's insistence on developing a website for it, although the enterprise was also a bit more work than they'd anticipated. They had only two rooms to rent out (couples preferred) and these were full much of the time, but both Ivor and Vera were surprised at how demanding, not to mention messy, otherwise pleasant guests could be. Not that they were unable to deal with matters; it was more a case of how little time they had left for themselves once the daily guests were breakfasted and sent on their way and the rooms prepared for the next set. They'd worked out a successful routine, with Vera cooking and Ivor playing jolly host and being responsible for laundry. But the routine invariably broke down whenever Coven's tiny police detachment felt challenged. To Vera, it seemed the detachment's policy, even before they made their own crime scene notes, was to call Ivor and ask if he'd "mind just taking a look."

It may have been Vera's growing annoyance, or it may have been her curiosity about the victim because he was the owner of a competing B&B in Coven, but when R. Guilford Ferren was discovered on the day before Michaelmas, slumped over the desk in his library, dead of a gunshot wound to the right temple, Vera announced that if Ivor Noonam was accepting the invitation to "just take a look," she, Vera Noonam, was going along to take a look too.

Ivor had made a half-hearted effort at dissuading her. "From what the young constable described," he'd tried to point out, "it sounds like a suicide. Surely you don't want to see that. It's not … it's not …" He didn't bother to finish the sentence, and instead stepped back to the little anteroom at the rear of the cottage to fetch an umbrella for Vera and one for himself. Several days later he reflected that it may have been the rain that put Vera into such a determined mood, but for the moment he was prepared to accept anything to keep the peace. As it turned out, Vera, once she'd fought down the shock and nausea at the sight of the late R. Guilford Ferren, had determined even before Ivor did that the odds were extremely high their competitor had met his untimely end at the hands of someone else and not his own.

Neither Ivor nor Vera knew the man. In fact they'd seen him only once that they could recall. Although Coven was a small village where inhabitants knew one another well enough to win bets on what neighbors were serving for dinner, Ferren was a recluse. While owning a bed and breakfast seemed a strange undertaking for someone who doesn't like people, Ferren's operation, significantly larger than the Noonams', was completely managed by his daughter and son-in-law.

If Vera's curiosity about the case included having a good look at their competitor's B&B, she was to be disappointed, for she and Ivor were met at the garden gate by the young constable who had telephoned and ushered directly into the library via a side entrance. Ferren was indeed slumped over his desk, dead of a gunshot wound as reported. The only new information immediately apparent was the revolver in his right hand, which Ivor immediately recognized as a military issue, .38 caliber Webley, but which to Vera was merely a "dreadful gun."

The desk faced the only entrance to the library, so both Noonams stood in the doorway for several minutes taking in the scene. It was an exceptionally large desk, taking up much of what was a rather small room to begin with. As might be expected of a recluse, there were no chairs in the room other than the one currently responsible for bearing the body of the late R. Guilford Ferren. Although both Noonams concluded almost immediately (Vera first) that this was no suicide, their initial scan of the scene picked up different impressions.

Ivor noted that the killer was almost certainly not a stranger, but quite likely not someone who knew Ferren intimately or else he — or she — would not have made such an obvious mistake. Vera, with what she later described as "a woman's eye," noted how impeccably clean and orderly the library was. There were no dust balls clinging surreptitiously to lamp cords or to the tassels at the bottom of the drapes, no books lying open on the shelves and no papers scattered about. Everything was in its place, neatly arranged at the proper angles, except for — almost offensively, Vera thought — the old-fashioned desk lamp. It had been bumped ever so slightly from its appointed position by the gun, and the lamp, in turn, had shifted a box of tissues so that it no longer stood in precise parallel to the edge of the desk.

Neither Vera nor Ivor spoke until they passed around either side of the desk to examine the rest of the room for possible clues. When they found none that were obvious, it was Ivor who broke the silence.

"It's rarely this obvious," he said, pre-empting a comment from his wife that solving crimes may not be as difficult as she had been led to believe all these years. Whether or not Vera accepted the point, Ivor could not be sure, for she simply nodded, something she'd always done throughout their many years of happy marriage whenever her opinions collided with what she was being told. However, several days later, when they learned that an electrician in a neighboring village had been arrested for the murder of R. Guilford Ferren, Vera did announce to Ivor that henceforth, when he was invited to come and "just take a look," she would be going along.

Why do both Vera and Ivor conclude that R. Guilford Ferren's death is not a suicide? How did Vera's "woman's eye" contribute to that conclusion? Why does Ivor determine that the killer is not a stranger but, at the same time, not someone who knew Ferren well?

Solution on page 177

17

Corinne Beardsley's Deadly Mistake

The secret, she knew, was always to be inconspicuous. Not that she needed to be reminded. There was reminder enough in the big, black Citroën parked at the opposite corner of Place Saint Pierre. The two men in the front seat were Gestapo and made no effort to conceal the fact. They'd be more than normally suspicious too these days, for everyone knew the invasion was coming any time now. Here in Caen, the atmosphere wasn't quite as jittery as elsewhere because just about everyone was convinced the Allies would hit the beach farther to the northeast, at Calais. Corinne herself believed that, even though her mission was here in Normandy.

She stepped off the curb onto the cobblestones of the square, head down, resisting a powerful urge to look at the Citroën. Be inconspicuous, she told herself. Be ordinary. Be just another war-weary, French housewife struggling to get through one more bleak and difficult day.

Behind the car, the bells of Ste. Étienne began tolling the noon-day Angelus. She stared lovingly at the twin spires of the old abbey and could barely resist a grin at the irony. Thirteenth century these spires were, looming some 90 meters over the square. The irony, Corinne understood better than most, was that this traditional Catholic call to prayer still prevailed in a city that had been strongly Protestant for over 300 years. If asked, Corinne could have added that Ste. Étienne dated back to the 11th century, that it was a fine specimen of Norman Romanesque architecture, and that the body of William the Conqueror had rested in its high altar until it was spirited away during the French Revolution.

Indeed there was very little about Caen and Ste. Étienne that Corinne didn't know, one of the reasons she was here. Three years before the war began — it seemed more like a century ago now — Corinne Beardsley, *Professor* Corinne Beardsley, had successfully defended her thesis on stress and balance in early Norman architecture. She would have been content to spend the rest of her life on the subject, but the day France fell she had been recruited by the Special Operations Executive, the SOE, as a radio operator. She would have been content too, spending the war in England doing her patriotic duty in that role, but a month ago the SOE had come to her again. As unpleasant as it might seem to her, they said, not to mention extremely dangerous, there was a medieval church building in Caen that had to be — their word was "eliminated" — for reasons she didn't need to know. No one would know how to do it better than Corinne Beardsley, they said. And so it developed that two nights ago, on the 3rd of June, a gray, single-engine Lysander had touched down in a dark field near St. Lo. It tumbled her out without ever coming to a complete stop, and then left her in the hands of the Resistance.

The Angelus bells continued as Corinne crossed the square, but it seemed the only sound in her ears was her own footsteps, growing louder and louder as she neared the Citroën. Then she realized that what she was hearing was her own heartbeat. And no wonder.

At the bottom of the shabby cloth bag hanging from the fingers of her left hand were folds of plastic explosive.

Corinne shifted the bag so that the rosary in her other hand could be seen more easily. It was important that she appear to be especially devout. She stopped for a second and stooped to scratch her ankle nonchalantly. It gave her a chance to take some deep breaths. Just a few seconds more and she would pass the car, pass the façade of Ste. Étienne, and then drop into the Church of Saint Pierre behind it. Here she would pray the Angelus like other women of the city and then remain to pray at every statue, to wander about with her rosary — and scout the building for its weak point, for the spot where the plastic could do the most damage.

As she passed the car, the two Gestapo agents got out almost casually. Even before they said anything, Corinne realized she had made a deadly mistake.

 What was Corinne Beardsley's deadly mistake?

Solution on page 178

18

After Hours at the Bank

The first thought that went through Max Shank's mind when he opened the door was that the four men who came into the bank were the weirdest looking bunch he'd ever seen. His second thought was a realization that he should not have opened the door at all and the third was *Holy Cow! They're going to rob the bank!*

Back to his first thought. The four men at the main entrance of Metro Savings & Loan were an odd lot to be sure, at least in appearance. The one who had impersonated the bank messenger, and so far the only one to do any talking, wasn't so much overweight as he was lumpy. And the extra pounds were all concentrated below his waistline so that he looked like a giant pear with feet. It didn't help either that the uniform jacket was too loose and the pants too tight.

Two of the others looked to Max like a bad version of Mutt and Jeff. One was a full head taller than Max, with a long face and extremely long arms and huge hands that hung down like saddle-bags. The other was a head shorter — a huge head, and it was completely bald. Both Mutt and Jeff carried large sports bags and although the contents were obviously very heavy it did not seem to occur to either of them to set the bags down once they were inside the bank. The fourth man was the only one whose body shape appeared close to average but anyone looking at him was inevitably drawn to long clumps of fiery red hair that stood out like airplane wings above both ears at precise right angles to the side of his head.

In sharp contrast to their physical differences, all four wore identical George W. Bush face masks. Jeannie, the teller, recognized these as coming from the giveaway bin at A Buck or Two out at the edge of town, but she wasn't able to explain that to Max until some time later.

Despite the unique appeal of their physical appearance, Max had little time to reflect on that, nor on his second thought — the fact that he'd opened the door to a night messenger without first checking his credentials, even though it was not their regular man. Instead, Max was totally absorbed by his third thought. These guys had come to rob his bank, and it was soon apparent that they'd done some advance planning. Not only did they know that the night messenger regularly arrived at 6:30 p.m., they also seemed to know that the same four bank employees worked late every second Thursday.

Once inside the bank all four had pre-assigned tasks. The phony night messenger, the one who soon made clear he was in command, was the only robber with a gun, a visible one anyway. By immediately putting its muzzle under the security guard's nose, he'd successfully persuaded that worthy to lie down in the manager's office and submit to being wound up like a mummy with duct tape. While that was happening, the fourth man — Max thought of him now as the Red Baron — herded Jeannie the teller and Wilma the assistant accountant into the same office, but in what appeared to be a gentlemanly gesture decided to leave them untied. The Red Baron then took up position in the manager's swivel chair, where he found particular delight in spinning himself around and around. The phony messenger, having exchanged his jacket and hat for that of the security guard, with Max in tow, took up the guard's normal post at the front door. It was the only portal through which the interior of the bank could be seen from the street and should a patrol car drive by — as happened twice — anyone looking in would have an unobstructed view of the back of a uniform, quietly on duty.

Mutt and Jeff meanwhile took their bags of tools back to the vault where the heart of the operation was to beat. Here the initial smoothness of the break-in experienced a few bumps. Mutt took a long power drill from his bag — Max needed only a second to realize that the safety deposit boxes were his target — while a heavy sledge hammer emerged from Jeff's. The rows of boxes could be seen behind a door of clear Plexiglas and it was this door that represented Jeff's first assigned objective. The little man rotated his shoulders one after the other, hefted the hammer and took a mighty swing at the center of the door. A major miscalculation as it turned out because the Plexiglas absorbed the blow and, like a slingshot, fired the hammer back at twice the speed. Instead of dropping it, Jeff clung to the hammer for dear life and was thus catapulted back into the lobby, skidding to a stop on the tile floor in front of the manager's office.

The Red Baron was so startled by the sudden arrival of a sledge hammer with his colleague in tow that he tipped the swivel chair over backward and landed in Wilma's lap. It was her scream that finally broke the spell and caused the messenger-now-guard to yell at Mutt to make Jeff swing at the *latch* on the door, at which point Max intervened to explain that the door wasn't locked anyway and simply had to be pulled open.

A second bump occurred when Mutt began drilling the locks on the safety deposit boxes and burned out two drill bits before he realized the tool was set on reverse. That would have been only a minor setback had the process not blown a fuse. The backup system came on immediately but with lighting only and no air conditioning so that Mutt and Jeff particularly had to work in increasingly stifling conditions, a factor that definitely slowed their progress.

It was about an hour later, with Mutt drilling and Jeff emptying the boxes into his sports bag — the two had stripped out several dozen boxes and had many more dozens to go — when the Red Baron suddenly appeared behind the messenger, his George W. Bush mask askew, and pleaded, "I'm hungry, Ollie, can't we send out for something?"

To Max, that was the dumbest thing that had happened yet, but the fact that the messenger, who'd been treating the other three like a cranky babysitter, received this quite calmly *and* did not react to being called "Ollie" convinced him it was part of the plan. Then, when Ollie summoned Jeannie, Max knew for sure, for Jeannie was asked what she normally ordered when they called the diner down the street for takeout around 9 o'clock. She told him it was almost always tuna on rye with a diet lemonade. Whereupon the messenger instructed her, "Well, you're gonna order two of those. Now what about these?" he added, nodding vaguely at Max and with his gun hand pointed at Wilma and the guard.

Jeannie told him as she was the one who normally phoned the diner and knew the usual orders. Once again she was told to order doubles of everything. Max couldn't help but be just a bit impressed. Obviously, in casing the bank the gang had learned that it was regular practice for the four overtimers to call out for food, so what the robbers were doing was duplicating normal behavior and rewarding themselves at the same time with a bit of nourishment.

Ollie watched through the open door of the manager's office as Jeannie phoned in the order with the Red Baron hovering over her. When she hung up, the Baron flashed ten fingers twice.

Ollie looked at his watch and muttered, "Twenty minutes," through the mask.

Fifteen minutes later he clapped his hands loud enough to get the Red Baron out of the swivel chair to close the office door. Mutt and Jeff caught the signal too and went into the office. Ollie motioned Max into a chair a few feet away, behind the drapes that covered the front window. He then bound Max's hands and feet to the chair with duct tape and covered his mouth too. Max understood that Ollie would be taking no chances when the takeout delivery arrived but was surprised that the police had not arrived by now. Could it be, he wondered, that the gang's inadvertent alarm had been missed? Or worse, misunderstood?

 What inadvertent alarm call has the gang sounded?

Solution on page 179

19

Analyzing a DJ

What I hate about winter in these eastern cities is they don't know what to do about a snowfall. The least bit of a dump and everything stops dead like a bomb hit or something. And they're all the same — New York, Toronto, Boston, Philly, Montreal — well, maybe not Montreal. I was there once — February I think it was — and they had this big dump. Snowed all afternoon and night and the next morning everybody was going about their business like nothing happened. No way anything happens like that here in Manhattan I'll tell you. Oh, I guess I should have told you: I'm a cop, well, technically not a cop in the way most people think; I'm a crime scene analyst, a CSA. We're the ones make cops look good, but don't try and tell them that.

Anyway, I get this call to a DJ this morning — that's a dumper-jumper — over on 89th near Central Park West. Ninety percent of the time with a DJ the detectives get into an argument about murder or suicide. It's why we call these cases dumper-jumpers and they always need us CSAs to settle things. See, usually it starts with somebody finding a body on the sidewalk or a parking lot or wherever.

And it looks like it come out a window or off the roof, something like that. Even if a drop is short, a body can get pretty messed up so it's often hard to tell if it was dumped, in which case you're talkin' murder, or if the vic decided to do a swannie off the roof all on her own. And you know, in suicides it's almost always *her* — in my experience anyway. Seems women tend to jump. Guys usually pick another way out of this mortal coil.

I'm getting off track here. Now, like I said, I got called to this DJ this morning. No big deal. It's my job. But you see we had this dump of snow last night. According to the weather weenies, it snowed heavy from about midnight to 4 a.m. or so. Hey now, wouldn't you like *that* job! Weather weenie, I mean. Forecaster! I mean, in what other job can you be *so wrong so often* and not get fired! Anyway, this time the information was correct because it was after the fact. Even an idiot can tell you how long it snowed after it's over. Sorry, I'm doing it again. I'll stick with the story.

Anyway, I'm called to this DJ but it takes me, like, forever, to get there. Like a dummy I signed out a car but it didn't take long to figure out that wasn't going to work with all the snow, so I took it back to the pool and got on the subway. Turns out I didn't get to the scene till maybe 9-ish. Not good, 'cause the 9-1-1 came in at a few minutes to 7 and the first pair of blues got there at 7:20. But then I used the same excuse everybody else did this morning: the snow. To be truthful there really wasn't all that much. About enough to come up to the top of your shoes. Where I grew up out west folks would barely have noticed, but here in New York, well ... Thing was, it was that heavy kind of snow. The flakes are sort of wet and clumpy. Stick to everything and when they pile up a bit, they're hard to walk through. And then to make things worse it turned cold after the snow fell so there was this sort of crust on top.

So anyway I get to the scene and what we got is a three-story brownstone. Not apartments; this is all one house. Money here. The vic is on the sidewalk, and pretty well everybody's concluded it's a jumper. A woman. (What did I tell you before?) Blanket over her of course, because there's a string of nosey neighbors on the street by now and the blues were doin' their job. When I lifted it for a first look I could see there was snow underneath her but none on top of her or in the folds of her nightgown. Maybe I should have mentioned that first — she was wearing only this flimsy, pink pajama thing. Anyway, it sure looked like she ended up out here on the sidewalk *after* the snow had stopped falling.

The body was pretty much splayed out, one leg in a pretty unnatural position. Now, it's not easy to tell from the position how far a body has fallen but, on the other hand, it wasn't hard to figure out she sure didn't come out here and lie down. Dump or jump, the body had come down a bit of distance. The autopsy will give us some detail on the trauma and maybe some clues as a result but that's not on till tomorrow. Not a big woman — average-average for sure. She — oh, her name is Lucinda Patnos. At first look I made her late 40s, early 50s. Turns out she's 61. What those plastic surgeons can do! Anyway, here she was on the sidewalk in a direct line with the balconies above her.

Oh yea, a little bit about the brownstone. Like I said, three story. There's a balcony on the third floor, facing the street. I found out in a few minutes this was the master bedroom. Right below that, the second floor has another sort of half-balcony, not the kind you sit on, more like a big window sill with a railing around it. My guess is they put plants there in the summertime and then open the glass doors when they have guests 'cause that's where the dining room is. On the bottom floor, just above street level, there's a pair of large windows with fancy glass that look like maybe they swing open like doors. These have bars over them. We're in New York, remember?

The first thing I did on the inside was check out the third-floor balcony. I would have started there anyway, but one of the blues filled me in right away on footprints up there that match the slippers the vic — Lucinda — had on. Pink slippers and one of the heels had this nick in it. No question the feet that laid the prints in the snow up there had those slippers on. In fact, if you stood where I did at the entrance to the balcony, you'd see why both the blues and the guys from homicide had pretty much made up their mind this was a jumper. The snow on the balcony was completely undisturbed except for three distinct prints leading out to the railing. And there was snow all along the railing except in one spot where she would have slid over.

I got to admit I was sure leaning toward a jump myself. Even more so when I talked to the husband, Orpheus. How do you like that name by the way? You know, I think — I really do — that if your parents give you a truly unusual moniker, you're going to grow up to be rich or a crook. Maybe both because they often go together. No really ... just look at ... Sorry, I'm getting sidetracked again. Anyway, Orpheus.

His story is that she was depressed and had been talking gloomy for some time. (You should see the truckload of pills in her medicine cabinet.) They'd been to a party the night before, got back at 11 and then decided to have another drink. Which they did but then they had another and soon got into a row over her brother. Seems this is an ongoing fight. She's got this good-for-nothing brother and, well, you can fill in the blanks. So Orpheus says that he went to bed about 2 but in the guest room on the second floor. Says whenever they scrap like this she gets the master bedroom and he moves out. Anyway, she pours another drink; he goes to bed; the next thing he knows is it's morning and there's shouting out on the street and, well, here we are.

Now like I said, I was leaning toward a jump myself. Orpheus is not a big guy. About the same size as her — Lucinda, I mean — and him hoisting her up and dumping her off the balcony wouldn't be the first thing comes to mind. Still, it wouldn't be all that hard once he gets her up over one shoulder. He wears her slippers, carries her out, does the dump, backs in, and goes down to the sidewalk and puts the slippers on her. Of course, she'd have to cooperate for all this. Or be dead. But see, the problem with this is if he goes out to put the slippers on there's more footprints to explain and the blues said when they got there, there were no footprints in the snow leading in or out of the house. Almost seemed it just *had* to be a jump. See what he did, and it almost fooled me, he killed her here in the house, in the brownstone. How he did it, we'll probably get that from the autopsy now that we know we're lookin' for it.

Pretty clever really. Those footprints on the balcony almost sold me. Oh, he made them all right, the footprints I mean, and he dumped her too. But not at the same time. If it wasn't for his one mistake ... On the other hand, maybe I'm just smarter than he is!

Apparently Orpheus has made a mistake that leads the CSA to conclude this is a "dump" and not a "jump." What is that mistake?

Solution on page 179

20

The Anthrax Plot

Dzerzhinsk, USSR, May 10, 1960: Ten-year-old Yuri Ivanovich Rykov is noticed by the commissariat in charge of education by attaining a score that is right off the scale on an IQ test. Subsequent testing confirms these results and through a series of coincidences, this young Russian boy comes to the attention of President Leonid Brezhnev himself.

Berdyans'k, USSR, September 1, 1960: Yuri is taken from his parents and enrolled in a highly secretive school run by the KGB. Here he is educated in a western European manner, learning western cultures and philosophies. The curriculum places special emphasis on economics and finance, and on language learning. Yuri becomes proficient in English, French and German with a fluency that does not betray a trace of accent.

Vienna, Austria, November 10, 1968: Having been thoroughly indoctrinated in the principles of world communism and trained in a wide range of skills useful in espionage, Yuri Rykov is inserted into western Europe during the chaos following a short-lived uprising in Czechoslovakia. Many young Czechs fled across the border into Austria at this time and most were housed in a refugee camp on the outskirts of Vienna. Yuri, however, is not treated as a refugee because he holds a French passport. He goes under deep cover with the name Guy-Paul Laurent. The manager of a multinational bank headquartered in Switzerland employs him in the international currency exchange department. Yuri (now Guy-Paul) stays under cover for 20 years. He does not marry, lives a low profile social life, and is entirely comfortable within the tightly closed ranks of the Swiss banking system. His career is quietly successful and he rises steadily in the hierarchy, each promotion usually requiring a move to a different country in Europe. By 1988 Guy-Paul has lived in seven different cities. Early in this year he is posted to Luxembourg City as president of the important branch there.

Nicosia, Cyprus, January 12, 1988: The Secretary-General of the United Nations, Javier Pérez de Cuéllar, completes arrangements for an unusual meeting to be held in Cyprus in the autumn. With the cooperation of the new Cypriot president, Georgios Vassiliou, the Secretary-General has succeeded in getting U.S. President Ronald Reagan and British Prime Minister Margaret Thatcher to agree to meet secretly in Nicosia with the incoming president of the USSR, Mikhail Gorbachev. There is absolutely no media awareness of this meeting and only the innermost circle of each leader knows anything about it. The purpose of the meeting is to discuss Gorbachev's wish to pursue a policy of *glasnost.*

Smolensk, USSR, February 1, 1988: The head of the most secretive branch of the KGB, the department that for years has been inserting and controlling agents in western Europe, dies suddenly of an apparent heart attack at his dacha on the outskirts of the city. He is replaced by an assistant who is strongly opposed to *glasnost* and who, coincidentally — or perhaps not so — is an illegitimate son of the late Vyacheslav Molotov, once the dreaded chief advisor to Stalin and a man noted for being the USSR's most uncompromising, anti-western champion of world communism. Two days later, bank president Guy-Paul Laurent, the former Yuri Rykov, receives a message. It is the signal he has been awaiting for almost 20 years. Yuri is to emerge from deep cover.

Luxembourg City, July 7, 1988, 7:10 a.m.: Yuri receives further instructions. A recent addition to a safety deposit box in his Luxembourg bank is a package of stationery and conference supplies impregnated with powder containing anthrax. Naturally, Yuri does not have access to the safety deposit box but an agent with the proper password and key will remove the package today during normal business hours. Yuri will then keep this package in his private office.

He is also to prepare for a second task. Each night at 11:48 p.m. an armored truck emerges from beneath the bank and goes through a stringent security check at a special exit. Most of the time the truck carries negotiable securities. Tonight there will be a very different cargo. Also tonight, the regular driver will fail to show and Yuri, in disguise, will drive in his place. Near the Luxembourg-France border, the truck will be met by a car whose driver will take the truck to Marseilles, where the cargo will go by ship across the Mediterranean to Cyprus. Yuri will use the car to return to Luxembourg to continue his role as Guy-Paul, the bank president.

Luxembourg City, July 7, 1988, 11:00 p.m.: While the special cargo is being loaded into the truck, Yuri carefully removes the wig he has worn for years — under it he is completely shaven — removes his contacts and dons glasses with dark frames. He also removes the false mustache he has worn since coming to Luxembourg, adds bulk to his eyebrows and inserts small cheek pads. He puts a cushion on the driver seat so the security guard at the checkpoint will have to look upward. Yuri is not a tall man.

Luxembourg City, July 7, 1988, 11:48 p.m.: The check through goes well in Yuri's opinion, but for one heart-stopping instant. As they approach the checkpoint the guard waves; he recognizes the truck and after all, it has appeared at the scheduled minute. Still, the guard looks Yuri over carefully. While papers are being thoroughly checked Yuri attempts to look bored. He has been practicing running his finger under his nose and sniffing in an uncouth manner. It is an unaccustomed behavior for him and he makes sure the guard sees this. He also lifts his cap and scratches his bald head several times, responding to the guard each time in Breton-accented French, not the sophisticated Parisian flow the bank's clients hear from Guy-Paul Laurent.

The bad moment comes when Yuri realizes that despite all the careful preparation he has not taken off his Rolex, something the guard notices in the same instant. Thinking quickly, Yuri explains that it's a cheap knockoff he bought in Marseilles and that seems to satisfy the guard who waves them through. The armored truck heads south to pick up the motorway that goes direct to Marseilles. The guard meanwhile phones ahead to a checkpoint where the truck will be pulled over and searched.

Despite his careful preparation, Yuri has made at least two errors. What are they?

Solution on page 180

21

Assessing the Risk

Everything about the place looked normal. Just the way a rustic hide-away was supposed to look. In fact, Penny's first impression was that with a covering of snow and a few more tall pines or spruce behind it, the cabin would be an ideal focal point for a Christmas scene, a Currier and Ives print maybe. She didn't take time to enjoy the thought, however. There was no room for nostalgia on this mission, not if the ambassador's little girl was inside.

"Agent Lovatt!" Penny's radio tech called her softly from the ditch on the other side of the long laneway.

Penny stood up, confident that on her side of the lane the grass was tall enough to hide her from the cabin. "They're in position?"

The tech raised himself enough to make eye contact and held up his receiver. "Blue Team's in place. Mackie says there's a porch runs right across the back of the cabin. One step up from grade. He figures three seconds max to the back door from where they are in the trees."

"Tell 'em stand by," Penny ordered, and lowered herself below the rim of the ditch. There was no time to lose but she knew from expe-rience that nothing could mess up a kidnap recovery faster than com-

mitting too soon. She'd wait for Red Team. They were taking up position on the northwest side, where the trees were thicker and closer to
the cabin.

She raised herself one more time and leaned forward just far
enough to reach out and part the growth of couch grass that hid her
from the cabin. If only she knew the source of the tip that told them
the snatchers brought Ambassador Grelo's kid to this cabin. Like every
single member of the emergency response team, Penny was deeply
distrustful of anonymous tips and this one was especially trouble-
some. HQ was dead certain the kidnap was political. It was three days
old already and there'd been no ransom demand. Kidnappers looking
for money tend to act fast to score what they can before police get
resources organized. The political types — well, publicity's their game,
publicity and vengeance, and if anything, with his reputation,
Ambassador Grelo would fit the vengeance part perfectly. He wasn't
exactly a hero in his home country. Not that he was much admired
here either.

Carefully, Penny spread the opening in the couch grass a bit wider,
resisting the urge to swat the gnats buzzing at the back of her neck. Yet
again, she carefully took in the scene, still trying to work out what
was bothering her. Location? The cabin was definitely out of the way.
For sure she wouldn't be in this out-of-the-way spot had it not been for
the anonymous tip. It was simply too far away from the kidnap scene
to be part of a general search. Yet for the snatchers, it was close enough
to stay tuned in to the action. No, probably not the location. Still ...

So was it the setting? She stared at the cabin. It was at the end of a
long lane that angled awkwardly off the lightly traveled gravel road
behind her. The cabin was set back far enough — Penny counted nine
evenly spaced utility poles — so that it couldn't be seen from the
road, not without effort anyway. You had to be local to know it was
there. As it was, the locals weren't much help. Nobody knew the

owner. "Some guy from the city," was all they could offer and there hadn't been time for Penny or her team to dig any deeper.

As for the cabin itself: too cute to be real, she wondered? The log construction was definitely contemporary. Faux pioneer style and certainly a recent job. With her free hand, Penny raised binoculars and confirmed yet again that the roof was cedar shake and the shutters were vinyl. Along the northwest side, a stone chimney confirmed even further that the building was new. She followed the line of the chimney from the ground to the roof where smoke hung lazily in the windless sky. There was no way a pioneer could have found stones so perfectly matched in size. Although she couldn't see from where she hid in the ditch, the quality of the chimney and the shutters meant the windows were up to date too. That meant triple-glazed likely. Not the kind of window a response team can break through easily. When they went in — *if* they went in — it would have to be through the doors. The doors, the front one anyway, was ...

"Red Team, Agent Lovatt!" This time the tech slid on his belly over to her side of the laneway. "You were right! No door on their side but they can be at the front — they estimate two seconds. Is it go?"

Penny took several slow breaths. She raised the binoculars for another lingering look.

"Tell them stand down! Got that? *Stand down!* It's booby-trapped! Gotta be! I'm sending in the robot camera."

Why does Penny suspect a booby trap?

Solution on page 180

The Unlamented Demise of Tony "the Heaver" Pellino

People who didn't know him might easily have thought Tony "The Heaver" Pellino a model citizen. And reasonably so. He didn't drink, didn't smoke, and was ever faithful to his long-time girlfriend, Adele. He didn't disturb his neighbors, paid his taxes, drove within the speed limits and in the matter of social graces was a complete gentleman. The only thing wrong with Tony was that he killed people. It's what he did for a living. To be entirely accurate, Tony was only *suspected* of being a hit man for he'd never actually been caught. Still, that's not entirely accurate either: he'd been caught, several times in fact, but never convicted. Whenever a hit went down with the Heaver's signature all over it (according to city homicide, he was a "master carver," a knife man), Tony always had an unshakable alibi, a rock solid backup that frustrated the police and the prosecuting attorney's office beyond measure.

Therefore when Tony himself ended up at the receiving end of a murder for hire on a chilly, rain-soaked afternoon in the early spring of 1984, neither homicide detectives nor the prosecuting attorney were inclined to burn up the tracks with an intense investigation.

That was in spite of the luxury of an immediate suspect by the name of Barker Fritz-Lane. Barker would have been on the list to be questioned in any case because he and Tony had shared a bitter hatred that began years before in the St. Ignatius Boys' Home where they'd been raised. However Barker's name shot up to the top of the list when a neighbor reported seeing a man fitting his description in the elevator of Tony's apartment the day of the murder. As it turned out, the police found it, well, almost amusing that despite this and other clues pointing to Barker, he had an alibi — the same kind of "I was elsewhere, just ask so and so" escape that had always insulated Tony. "So and so" in Barker's case was a waitress at a pub known as the Jolly Miller where, he explained, he was a regular.

The city's newspapers treated Tony the Heaver's untimely end pretty much in the same casual way the police had. The leading daily buried it in the City Scenes section between a brief account of the mayor's Thanksgiving plans and an announcement about upcoming road construction. The tabloids gave it a bigger run because Tony had been dispatched somewhat creatively. His killer had tied him up in his own bathroom, his feet inside the toilet, hands strapped to his ankles with tape. The position was painful and made breathing difficult and, in a particularly vicious touch, Tony's asthma medication was hung from the ceiling just out of reach. Without his meds to keep the air passages open, Tony the Heaver had simply heaved away until he suffocated.

Initially, the police had tried to keep this piece of juicy information quiet but some earnest digging by a reporter for one of the tabloids, a junior on the city beat named Marisa Letto, had made it public almost immediately. What the detectives didn't realize was that Marisa was now about to write a piece for the Saturday edition that would turn their slow investigation on its ear.

Naturally, she'd spoken to the Jolly Miller waitress, Barker's alibi, at length. Not a difficult interview for the lady quite enjoyed the notoriety. After explaining that, yes, she had spent the whole afternoon in question with Barker right here in the Miller ("I was workin' afternoon shift, see.") she wanted to know if Marisa thought a good picture beside the article would help with her real career as an exotic dancer. Marisa explained she had no control over pictures but that didn't seem to bother the waitress. By the end of the interview, Marisa had learned that "Barker, he's my best fan, see," that "Sometimes I dance jus' for him," and that although the pub was pretty busy on the day of the murder, "I got ta sit down with him, see, 'tween servin' other customers 'cause the manager wasn't here." Marisa also learned — in far too much detail — that the manager was having an affair, that everybody thought he was a creep anyway, that work breaks were scheduled willy-nilly and that the pay was ... "Well, if it wasn't for Barker, see, I'd be jus' gettin' by."

Tony's neighbor was as forthcoming as the waitress: "Two-fifteen I saw a stranger in the elevator. He got on before I did. Rode up with me. I got out on the fourth and he went higher. Now I can't honestly remember whether the button for the fourth was lit when I got in, but he punched seven after I got on." Marisa was told with great certainty that "The guy's just over six feet. His head was same height as that little sign, you know, the one they always have that tells you who owns the elevator and that. My husband is the same height; that's how I know. And like I told the police, a mustache, glasses, and a pretty big tummy."

In contrast, Tony's girlfriend, Adele, was more than a bit reluctant to speak: "Why would you want to talk to me?" and reflective: "One day your man is there; the next he's gone." Her sadness and her grief had almost made Marisa want to cry. "Sure I knew Barker. No, they didn't like each other. Should have, though. Both orphans, both got real bad asthma, both from St. Ignatius. But what's the difference now? Tony's gone."

On the way over to her editor's desk with the Saturday edition piece in her hand, Marisa wondered whether what she'd put together would make Adele feel better or worse.

 Marisa Letto has put together information that should, at the very least, prod the police into investigating Barker Fritz-Lane more aggressively. What is that information?

Solution on page 181

23

A Perfect Crime?

I killed my wife this morning during the 8 o'clock news. Strangled her. To be perfectly honest, it was a lot easier than I had imagined. Not the actual doing it; that was no trouble at all. I was going to use the cord from her precious Tiffany lamp — there would have been some justice in that. Then I decided on a piece of rope, but in the end I just used my hands. No, doing it was easy. You see, what I was worried about was whether I could actually *do* it. In my head, I mean.

Oh, I've been thinking about it for, well, for years I guess. Almost from the beginning. I can't be sure I actually started on our wedding night, but probably I did. Probably I started when she picked up and walked out of our suite at The Grand and went down to the desk and booked herself a separate room. Still, as much as a person *wants* to kill someone, there's a long stretch between just thinking about it and those few seconds when all of a sudden it's real. That's why I'm surprised at how little I hesitated when the time came.

She was just sitting there like always, a couple steps from the TV screen. Everything exactly the same as it's been every single day after day after day after day! Coffee cup on the side table sitting in precisely the same spot — same cup every day too — arms crossed at the wrist and resting in her lap, hair a mess. And her mouth hanging open! *Always the mouth hanging open!* You have no idea ... Well, maybe you do. Doesn't matter. Maybe the mouth is what made it easy. Anyway it's over. It's what ... five hours ago now? Could be the explosion has already happened by now. Doubt it though. The way I figured, it's got to take most of the day for the gas to fill the house.

I can sense you're starting to frown. After all, a guy kills his wife you can hardly be expected to approve. But just hear a bit of my side of it before you pass judgment. I already told you about the wedding night; well, that's never changed. Gives you a pretty good overview, doesn't it? If nothing else, it explains why we never had kids, but in the overall picture that was pretty minor, really. Better that way in fact.

And now that it's finally over, even some of the ugly stuff doesn't seem as important as it did at the time. Like the Tiffany lamp I mentioned? It's been sitting on the piano for years — her mother's piano but that's another story. You see, I'd been saving money bit by bit over months for a really decent camera. It's tough in those early days, isn't it, when you're just getting your life going? And she never worked — her mother didn't think it was "fitting." That's what she said! "Not *fitting*!" Anyway, with only one income it takes a while to pull together the kind of cash you need for something extra but I finally did it. I know, you've put two and two together already and you're right. She took the money one day while I was at work and bought the Tiffany lamp!

I remember that was the time I finally decided once and for all to do this. In fact I almost did it then and probably should have! They'd have caught me though, the police, because I didn't have a plan. But that was, what ... 24 years ago? I'd be out of jail by now! Anyway, that's water under the bridge, but it gives you a feel for what it's been like, doesn't it? Besides, this time I had a plan and it's foolproof.

But I'm getting ahead of myself. You have to understand the worst part. Like the coffee cup — the *same* coffee cup in the *same* spot every morning. And the 8 o'clock news. On the same channel every time. Even the volume set the same! That's what it's been like all these years. And then after the 8 o'clock news, it's one egg over easy and two pieces of brown toast, no butter and the crusts cut off. And heaven forbid anybody interferes because at 8:30 comes the morning show. Then precisely at 9:31 the phone rings. Her sister Leila. The sister-in-law from hell. It's her twin by the way. Peas in a pod. Get this. She phones, Leila does, to ask if it's okay if she drops in. There's no question it's okay! She comes every single day! At 11 o'clock! That puts a *double* dose in the house then and you should hear the conversation. The same script every day. They should have taped it. Could save the effort of opening their mouths. Every once in a while, but only in nice weather, they'd rope in the mailman for a chat. He never seemed to mind but then he's just as dull.

I never actually had to put up with the Leila torture until I retired some years ago. Well, I didn't really retire — no way I'd stay home by choice. Truth is, I was let go in one of those mergers. Knocked the skids out of me. But back to Leila. In a way I owe her for my plan because for one, I had to figure out a way to do this on a day when she wouldn't be here. And for two, since that would be a rare day indeed, I'd be forced to act if it ever happened. No procrastination! See, what I'd worked out is that if I did it during the 8 o'clock news, I'd have the whole day for the gas to seep out once I loosened the fitting down at the furnace.

There's two stairways to the basement, see, because it's an older house. Her mother's house — I didn't mention that did I? She's been gone for years so I guess my luck's not all bad. Anyway the stairs. I leave both doors open so after the basement fills up the gas comes up and fills the rest of the house. Now just to the left of the TV is a gas fireplace. All I have to do is make sure the pilot light is on. Once there's enough gas in the room — then, well, boom! The whole house goes up and away blows the evidence. And what doesn't blow up burns up. A tragic accident while the bereaved husband is very visibly meeting with his investment advisor, then the dentist, and then sniffing around a dealership for a new car. Got to be out all day.

Can't remember how long I waited for Leila to finally go away somewhere but miracle of miracles, yesterday she left for Vancouver. See, Leila was married once. Only six months before the guy took off but she had a son. He's grown now and smart enough to live at the opposite end of the country. So for me, well, this morning was a case of opportunity knocks and there you have it!

I know you're probably wondering why I didn't just leave years ago, or get a divorce, maybe why I even married her in the first place. Reasonable questions I suppose. As for the last one, I think you've got to be my age to really understand how dumb you can be when you're young. As for leaving or divorcing, I don't know. Inertia I guess. Look at how long it took me to actually do away with her. Anyway, you figure it out. I'm going to start enjoying myself.

The narrator has described his plan as "foolproof" but there is potential for glitches. What are the possible weaknesses in his perfect crime?

Solution on page 181

24

Mr. Mayo's Wakeup Test

Only three students in Mr. Mayo's senior English class had even a vague idea how to pronounce his real name (it was Salvatore Luciano DiMastromontellamayo) and none of them at all had the foggiest idea how to spell it. Their conviction — for it was conviction, handed down over the years and elevated now, beyond the status of myth — was that other than Mr. Mayo himself, only his mother could spell it. The students knew his name had 16 syllables — that was common knowledge. They also knew that Mr. Mayo had been born and raised in Switzerland where he grew up speaking Italian, German and French; that he had lived in Aberdeen, Scotland, for ten years where he'd learned to speak English with a Celtic burr; and that after marrying a Canadian girl from Calgary (who kept her own surname because she too didn't relish the challenge of spelling, or even pronouncing, DiMastromontellamayo) he'd moved to northern Arizona because the red hills reminded him of Tuscany where, curiously, he'd never been!

In fact, except for the mystery surrounding his name, the students in senior English knew and regularly exchanged quite a lot of information about Mr. Mayo. In part, they did that because he was an element in their lives that they all had in common. Partly, it was because students love to compare notes about their very best and very worst teachers (Mayo was one of the former) and because the students in senior English had the good fortune to begin every school day in Mr. Mayo's class. It was well-established lore at Woodrow Wilson Composite High School that if you were not fully awake when the morning bell signaled the beginning of the school day, the first five minutes with Mayo would cleanse your brain of even the stickiest cobwebs.

Quite simply, this outcome was a product of Mr. Mayo's effervescent personality. There was no room for drowsiness or inattention in whatever space he happened to occupy. It was also because he began every single class with a brief test. Nothing so mundane and ordinary as a pop quiz, but rather a mental challenge, a puzzle, a conundrum. Often, but not invariably, these twisters were built around some tricky element in English usage and grammar. Another important thing the students understood about Mr. Mayo was that he not only knew all there was to know about the complexities of the English language — and loved every one of them passionately — he was committed to exposing and correcting every perceived violation of proper usage and to herding all his students along that same path. That's why the responses to the morning test on Thursday, February 19, veered directly to a consideration of language for the solution.

The test, delivered orally by Mr. Mayo, went like this:

Pietro cuts an apple in half while making lunch for his sister, Luciana, and asks which piece she would prefer.

Luciana, who is quite a bit younger than her brother, pipes enthusiastically, "The biggest half!"

The older child smiles indulgently, for he loves his little sister, and replies, "You mean the bigger half."

Who is correct here, Luciana or Pietro?

Junior Clarkson jumped in ahead of everyone else in the class. His choice was "bigger," and before he could clearly articulate his reasoning, about three-quarters of the group chimed in with their support, so if Junior did in fact offer an explanation for his choice, no one heard it.

A smaller contingent opted for "biggest." This contingent was led by Callista Verben, a consistent "A" student whose answers usually attracted a following because of her reputation for high achievement.

As it turned out, both answers were wrong, a major embarrassment for Junior and Callista. Also, as it turned out, "Ditzy" Lukash, normally a full-time occupant of the bottom of the bell curve, would have offered the right answer had she managed to get to school that day before noon. (She had awakened firmly convinced it was Saturday and took the bus to her weekend job at Wal-Mart.) When the test question was repeated to her just after lunch, she gave the correct response right away.

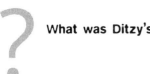 **What was Ditzy's answer?**

Solution on page 182

25

Mr. Mayo's Wakeup Test: A Sequel

As a direct consequence of Mr. Mayo's ever-popular wakeup tests, "Ditzy" Lukash risked losing her nickname forever during the second week of the spring semester. Although no one thought to question him on the matter, a subtle shift in the nature of Mr. Mayo's wakeups had been taking place since about the middle of winter term. The change was more of a gentle drift than an abrupt turn, but it was significant nevertheless. Although his passion for the English language, or rather for stamping out careless usage, had not diminished one whit, throughout the winter term Mr. Mayo's wakeups had been gradually sliding away from issues of language to occupy a wider and more diverse canvas. One unanticipated result — certainly unanticipated by Mr. Mayo — was the sudden illumination of hitherto hidden ability in Ditzy Lukash.

Sometime after spring term ended, when Mr. Mayo had an idle summer to reflect on the previous academic year, he wondered whether Ditzy's long-established reputation as an airhead might have simply been a product of her very casual attendance record at Woodrow Wilson Composite High. What made him contemplate this possibility was his recall of the day he had, for the first time ever, presented a wakeup test dealing exclusively with numbers. As the students filed in that day he had written the number nine on the chalkboard four times, thusly: 9 9 9 9.

"I want you to take these nines," he had said into the customary din of books being dropped to the floor, chair legs scraping and low chatter, "and make them equal 100. No limits. Any method is acceptable. You've got three minutes!"

To his complete surprise, Ditzy turned the nines into 100 in only a few seconds. Later that day in the faculty lounge, Mr. Mayo's colleagues, even the math teachers, took several minutes to get the answer.

The very next day, Mr. Mayo's surprise deepened to shock after Ditzy was way out in front again. This day's wakeup had dealt with letters of the alphabet. He told the class to insert the missing letters G, H and I in the proper place in the diagram he was about to draw. He then drew a horizontal line across the chalkboard at the front of the room, entering uppercase letters in block form so that the finished product looked like this:

$$\underline{\text{A} \qquad \text{EF} \qquad \text{KLMN} \qquad\qquad \text{T} \quad \text{VWXYZ}}$$
$$\text{BCD} \qquad\qquad \text{J} \qquad\quad \text{OPQRS} \quad \text{U}$$

Not only was Ditzy far ahead of the class solving this one, she had even walked to the front of the room unbidden to write her answer on the board! Although Mr. Mayo was most definitely pleased by what appeared to be a grand awakening, he could barely suppress a mild suspicion that there might be more to the situation here than met the eye, an uncomfortable feeling reinforced by the fact that Ditzy had actually been in class two days in a row now, not just on time but early!

His suspicion diminished somewhat when he discovered that Ditzy was no longer working at Wal-Mart, a development which, if nothing else, went some way toward explaining why she was suddenly finding her way to school on a regular basis. It seems that at the very busiest point on a Red Sale Saturday, Ditzy had overloaded a warehouse-only dolly with plastic garbage pails, then, contrary to store policy and safety regulations, not to mention the laws of physics, had opted for a short cut through the store. When the load came crashing down, she had been passing through the glassware department.

Any lingering suspicions Mr. Mayo may have harbored about Ditzy's skills disappeared on Friday of the second week of spring semester, for on that day he deliberately introduced a distractor into the morning wakeup that he'd never used before: Roman numerals. He'd enhanced the day's test with a bit of artwork so that what students saw projected on the drop screen when they entered that day was a quite convincing drawing of an old gravestone, complete with what looked like lichen growing in the text.

Revere the memory of
Piper Thomas Mann
who departed this earth
XXII May MDCCLII
in the
XCVth year of his life
& his devoted widow
Rebecca Jane Bridger
who on IX June MDCCXLIII
entered the hereafter
at age LXXXIV

Ditzy spotted the error on the gravestone before Mr. Mayo even posed the challenge to the class. Interestingly, in what was clearly an act of sensitivity toward her somewhat bewildered English teacher, she whispered her observation to him while the class was still settling down.

Having thus proven herself, Ditzy made every attempt through the remainder of the semester to keep a low profile. She had become comfortable with the nickname over her teenage years and, perhaps more important, was anxious to keep her real name a secret. Her parents, life-long hippies, had named her Turtle Dove when she was born.

What are Ditzy's answers to Mr. Mayo's three wakeup tests?

Solution on page 182

26

Leo's Interim Report

Cal,

Just got your message on my voice mail. Sorry! Didn't realize this case is urgent. Am waiting for the _official_ report from the weather service (see CHED excerpt below for now). I've also attached pieces from the file so you can see it's not a suicide. Proper report to follow in 48 hours at the outside.

Leo

From writeup by Constable Sabapathy

21/01/2006

Re: <u>Albert Basinchuk</u>, deceased: Whitsun Road, RR #4, Strathmore, Alberta. In response to 9-1-1 call from rural mail deliverer, <u>Berniece Laviere</u>, logged at 11:40 a.m., 19/01/2006, undersigned attended scene at address above. Found subject Basinchuk at wheel of 1996 Ford Taurus. No vital signs. Strong indication of carbon monoxide poisoning (cherry red lips etc.;

see coroner's report). Evidence indicates subject Basinchuk backed car out his laneway, stopped at junction with road and left motor running until he expired. Car in *Park*, ignition on, gas tank empty. Pending further investigation and/or submission of evidence to the contrary, preliminary conclusion is self-inflicted death. (Transcripts of Berniece Laviere interview attached. See also coroner's report.)

From coroner's report

<u>Summary</u>: Subject is white male, DOB 25/12/1933, 145 lb., 5'7", in reasonable health for the age but moderate to serious arthritis evident. Old injury to right shoulder suggesting limited use of the right arm. Body shows no visible signs of trauma. No evidence of coronary or stroke.
COD: carbon monoxide poisoning.
TOD: c. 10 to 11 a.m. January 19, 2005.
Interim ruling: presumed suicide. <u>No autopsy performed.</u>

From the noon news & weather on CHED-AM for Jan 19.

"Hey, they don't call Calgary the world capital of chinooks for nothing, but this latest contribution from Old Man Winter — or should it be Old Man Summer? — beats all, doesn't it? If you were driving to work early this morning you don't need to be told that the heavy wet snow we got after midnight was right up over your winter boots if you were smart enough to be wearing them. But then the chinook! Wow! According to our buddy Gene at the weather office, the temperature jump between about 9:15 and 10:30 was a mind-blowing 19 degrees! With just enough rain too, to make you wish you'd left those boots on. Well, you can put them in the closet for the next couple of days 'cause old buddy Gene says the warm stuff is going to stay with us ...

From transcript of interview of Laviere

Normally, I do Rural Route 4 in the morning, you know. There's only three boxes on Whitsun Road but it's long and winding, you know, so it takes me about 15 minutes. Usually I hit it around 9, 9:15, never later. 'Cept if there's trouble, like the snow on Friday, the day I found old Albert, you know. See, he's always waiting for me out at the road in his car. Never misses. You know what old guys are like. 'Course I was real late that day. See, the plows clear the roads real early and all that but I usually don't start till I know they're pretty well finished. Had one of them hit me once, you know. Anyway, old Albert. Almost noon when I got there and seen him in the car. Scared the ... I mean, it was really scary. Looked like he was dead, you know. And my cell doesn't work out there. Had to drive out to the highway.

Leo still has to submit a final and more formal report, but he has concluded that Albert's death is not a suicide. Why?

Solution on page 183

27

An Enemy Within?

Five consecutive days of rain and mist had brought some relief to the defenders in the castle. The misery that came with being cold and soaked to the skin was more than compensated for by the fact that the penetrating dampness had also softened the ropes on the mighty catapults ranged on the other side of the moat. For five days, the English engineers had been unable to launch huge stones against the castle walls or drop kegs of burning pitch from the sky. And for the first time since the siege began in November, Sir Guy de Taillebourg had enjoyed a sound sleep. Being rudely awakened from this pleasant slumber accounted, at least in part, for his present foul mood, but the reasons for it went much deeper than that.

To begin with, Sir Guy had been awakened to be told that Pierre-Paul, his faithful and dependable squire, was dead. And not dead from battle or from manning the ramparts. Although it was an English arrow, a "clothyard," buried deep in his chest, Pierre-Paul had been killed — murdered — by someone inside the castle. Sir Guy's sense of logic suggested otherwise, but deep down in his gut he truly wanted to believe that his new ally, the dark English archer, was the murderer. Then, with no risk whatever to his immortal soul he could have the Englishman taken to the dungeon below and tortured until his screams terrified the army ringing the castle.

There was good reason for him to seek that kind of vengeance. The man, after all, was the enemy. Yes, the archer had fought hard and well thus far for Sir Guy, and yes, the explanation for fighting his own people — that his family had been dispossessed and then executed by the Earl of Stowe — was nothing unusual. Still, he was the enemy. The archer was English. Not only that, he was one of the cursed longbowmen who, only five months before, had devastated the cream of French nobility at Crécy. Fifteen times on that muddy plain the French knights had obeyed the command of their king, Philip VI, and charged the English line. And each time they failed, their dead and wounded pierced by the blizzard of arrows launched by English bowmen.

Philip himself had barely escaped and fled to Amiens, while the English army led by their king, Edward III, had burned and pillaged its way north and was now laying siege to Calais. Sir Guy had survived the debacle at Crécy, but not unscathed. An English arrow had pierced his mail as if it were freshly churned butter while another had killed his horse. He'd had the good luck to fall unconscious under his dying charger and thus was missed by the foot soldiers scavenging the field after the battle, bashing in the heads of the wounded and stripping them of armor. Then, a mere two weeks after he'd returned to his estate at La Roche-Darrien, the shame of defeat still hanging over him like a black cloud, the Earl of Stowe's army had appeared outside the walls.

Sir Guy stood by the lifeless body of Pierre-Paul and gazed through the dim light toward the parapet above the drawbridge. That was where the English archer was stationed. In fact, with his longbow always at hand, he had been there since the siege began, stubbornly refusing any offers of relief.

"Looking for a clear shot at the Earl," he had explained. "Just one clear shot."

Sir Guy had agreed readily. He knew from experience just how accurate the English longbowmen could be and over what great distances their arrows were lethal, and he realized that this mysterious archer was the only one of his kind and skill among the castle's defenders. He also knew that the span between the parapet and the dung heap where Pierre-Paul's body now lay was at the outer edge of a longbow's range, but for a practiced archer it was possible. Very possible.

The two men-at-arms who had shaken Sir Guy awake stood impatiently to one side, waiting for his decision. They knew their leader was wrestling with himself. An excuse to exact vengeance would be sweet. On the other hand ...

What logic tells Sir Guy de Taillebourg the English archer did not shoot the arrow that killed Pierre-Paul?

Solution on page 183

28

En Route to the Scene

Within seconds of climbing into the passenger seat of the Toyota Highlander, Calla Zentil knew she was going to have a bad day. She was well aware that visiting the accident site would help with the investigation into Eva Bench's insurance claim, but by the time she finished buckling her seat belt she was almost ready to just give Eva the benefit of the doubt. Some weeks before, Eva had completely totaled a Highlander like the one they were in now and her claim for neck and back injury was a large one. As the company agent assigned to the case, Calla would be the one to decide whether to accept or dispute that claim, normally a task she welcomed. But not this time, for Eva Bench was one of those people who didn't — or couldn't — shut up.

In the hour it took to get from the city to the country road where Eva had rolled her vehicle down an embankment into a dry creek bed, Calla had heard all about Eva's first marriage, about her scare with breast cancer, her disgust with the contractor renovating her kitchen and his indifference to her dust allergy, and had been treated to an overly detailed account of Eva's discussions with her teenage daughter about the trials and tribulations of life. Other than an occasional "Goodness!" and a few distracted "Oh my's," Calla had not been able to put in a word for 40 minutes, but when they turned east off the main highway out of the city, she jumped into a pause in the monologue.

"On this road? The accident?" she asked.

A burst of staccato responses came back. "Oh no. At least I don't think so. I mean, it's so-o-o confusing to me now. But this could be it. No! I turned off. I remember, like, this really big tree. It's so hard to remember, especially since the rollover. My therapist says it's repressed memory."

"There's a big tree just ahead there, at the top of the hill. It's a T intersection, so is it left or right?" Calla secretly congratulated herself for getting in two consecutive sentences. On topic too.

"Left, I'm almost sure. Yes, left! There are no signs or names for the roads around here, are there? But it was a gravel road. I'm positive about that. Hard, you know, when you've never been down a road before and then you have an accident that almost kills you."

At the intersection Eva turned left without signaling. "I'm going to want to stop soon," she said. "Take off this big collar. Jim — that's Doctor Jim Banks — he's a great buddy of my first husband, Corey. They go to Prince Edward Island every July for a week to golf. Jim's in his like, third marriage, can you believe? And he's only 40. Maybe 41. Gorgeous though! Jim says I can take off the collar for ten minutes every hour or so as long as I don't move around. Could aggravate the whiplash. It's so-o-o hot, the collar."

Eva slowed the Highlander as they approached a curve. "Jim's an ortho ... ped ... *pod*? Big bucks in that, Corey says."

Calla opened her mouth to speak but then took time to draw a deep breath and Eva had jumped to a new topic.

"Don't know what's so special about men and golf," she opined as she slowed and edged far to the right to negotiate a railroad crossing. "I've tried it. Like, with my girlfriends, I mean. Still doesn't seem ..."

"Swamp on both sides!" This time Calla interrupted without hesitation. And she wasn't about to yield the floor until she'd made her point. "The police report describes the area as a country road bisecting a swamp. Next is a long grade. *We're on it, the grade!* And then the ... That's it right there. It has to be, isn't it? Dry creek bed just off to the right! This is it, right?"

Eva pulled to a stop in apparent response to Calla's excitement. For the first time, she was silent but now tears began to well and her bottom lip pushed out in a little-girl pout. The silence continued for a few more seconds as she nodded slightly, pushing her chin against the rim of the collar.

"That's ... that's where the guy, the kid, came out of the trees on one of those, what are they called, ATVs?"

"All terrain vehicle," Calla filled in. "But this guy — or kid — took off, didn't he? We've no idea who he is."

"He was, like, crossing the road. Really fast. Maybe he doesn't even know that I ... See, as soon as I saw him, that's, like, when I swerved. To miss him. And then the next thing I remember is waking up at General with Chuck holding my hand and this nurse shining a light in my eyes."

Eva dabbed at her eyes with a tissue. "Have you seen enough now? Can we go? I want to go home and talk to my therapist, to Louis. This is so, like, *awful*."

On the way back to the city, it seemed to Calla that Eva returned to form in very short time. On this leg of the journey Calla learned all about the second husband, Chuck, and his firm belief in the design of Toyotas and why, if she had been in any other car she might easily have been killed in the rollover and that would be even more devastating to the insurance company Calla represented than the claim they were facing now. In addition to hearing all this, and despite being presented with lengthy dissertations on the challenge of second marriages and the benefits of at least one separate spousal vacation a year and the pros and cons of Botox, Calla was still able to retreat to a private corner of her mind briefly. She was feeling great satisfaction at her decision to visit the accident site and to have Eva drive there.

Calla Zentil has apparently discovered something that affects her opinion of Eva and Chuck's claim. What is that discovery?

Solution on page 184

29

A Discussion at Clancy, Goldberg & Associates

CLANCY: This is it? Just two files?

GERWAL: They're all you need.

CLANCY: Hmmpf ... What's this? A receipt for 18 dollars and 25 cents. Another one seven days later for 22 dollars. This one the next week for 19.50, another for 23. These belong to the Moskovitz woman, don't they? Here's one for 18.25. How did you get these?

GERWAL: That's not your concern. They're petrol station receipts. The ...

CLANCY: I might have been able to figure that out, Gerwal! They've got Irving Oil written across the top. And in this country you say "gas bar" or "gas station." This isn't England, you know.

GERWAL: I'm not from England.

CLANCY: Well, wherever it is you're from. All I ...

GERWAL: India. And not just India: the *Punjab*. Now do you want to discuss my heritage or do you want my report.

CLANCY: Okay, okay, Gerwal, don't get huffy. It's just ... well, when you're in Rome, you should talk like the Romans.

GERWAL: You mean like: *Braccae tuae aperiuntur*?

CLANCY: Don't get smart-alecky with ... with ... *Braccae tu ...* That's good, Gerwal! That's funny! *Braccae tuae aperiuntur.* You're telling me my fly is open. Where did you pick up Latin like that?

GERWAL: At school in the Punjab. I can give it to you in Greek too. But I remind you my fee is 500 a day, so do you want to talk about my investigation of this witness or do you want to play linguistic one-up?

CLANCY: Okay, okay. Now, the witness, this Mrs. Moskovitz that saw the accident. *Allegedly* saw the accident ...

GERWAL: The next receipt is the one you want.

CLANCY: The next ... hmmm ... yes. Twenty dollars even. 8:04 a.m. on November 12.

GERWAL: The accident was at 8:02.

CLANCY: Yes. And on Friday, November 12. Hmmpf ... This receipt is Irving Oil too. Might have known. And every receipt is from the gas bar at 240 King Street.

GERWAL: There are photographs of it in the other file. It's on the northeast corner of King and Queensgate Boulevard. Faces King.

CLANCY: Photographs? Oh, I see, yea. You took these?

GERWAL: Of course. The one you're looking at is the side view. I took it from the south side of Queensgate. Typical modern petrol ... er ... *gas* station. Three vehicle alleys parallel with the front of the building. Four pump islands, each with a back to back pump so they can handle up to eight vehicles at once. Self-serve on the left island, full serve on the right. There's a front view of the station there too. I took that from the west side of King so you can see ...

CLANCY: Aren't we getting a little information overload here, Gerwal?

GERWAL: When I investigate you get the full Monty.

CLANCY: The what?

GERWAL: Never mind. She ... the witness, Mrs. Moskovitz ... she lives three blocks east of the station. On a little cul-de-sac off Queensgate.

CLANCY: Probably accounts for why all these receipts are from the same place. She just runs up the street and ... What's this picture? Her car?

GERWAL: Yes. A Buick Century, 2003.

CLANCY: In good shape. Except for that little dinger there on the driver's side.

GERWAL: Dinger?

CLANCY: *Dent.* The dent there below the fuel door.

GERWAL: Dinger ... *dinger*! The things you do to the English language in this country!

CLANCY: When in Rome, Gerwal. I'd say if you look close you'd find a few more dingers like that too, given her age. By the way, that's something that bothers me. Here she's a pensioner with all the time in the world and she gets her gas in rush hour. Look at these other receipts ... 8:05 a.m., 8:28, like that. Always pays cash too.

GERWAL: She's an early riser. And regular as clockwork. Every Friday she gets gas and then goes grocery shopping. Do you want me to dig up even more on her lifestyle?

CLANCY: At 500 dollars a day?

GERWAL: My fee is a lot less than you'll be charging your client for legal services.

CLANCY: Yea, he could get burned if we can't shake this Mrs. Moskovitz, 'cause according to her, he ran the red light at Queensgate and T-boned the school bus going south on King. Didn't even touch the brakes.

GERWAL: But she didn't actually put it that way, did she?

CLANCY: No, what she told the police was that while she was at the pumps she saw our guy drive right into the intersection against the red light and that his brake lights never came on.

GERWAL: Of course, you ...

CLANCY: Yes, his car's been tested and the brake lights work so they must have been working on November 12 too.

GERWAL: Nevertheless, in my opinion you have more than enough here in these files to generate a large dollop of reasonable doubt when Mrs. Moskovitz takes the stand.

CLANCY: In fact I do, Gerwal, in fact I do. You've earned your fee. By the way: *dollop* — I like that! *Dollop!* That's good, Gerwal!

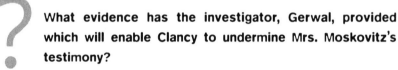

What evidence has the investigator, Gerwal, provided which will enable Clancy to undermine Mrs. Moskovitz's testimony?

Solution on page 184

30

An Alternative Career

The idea did not come to her with the sudden, light-bulb-flashing *AHA!* celebrated in seminars on creativity. Rather, Torrey's plan developed slowly throughout her studies as an art history major at Bransome Tech. She never did uncover just what ignited the initial spark; it could have been any one of a number of things. But for sure, once the spark was glowing, even if subconsciously, it was fanned into a flame during her final year, after a group of former students came to speak about their professional lives since graduating from Bransome.

A very few had become curators of public galleries; Torrey noted that, without exception, they were by far the oldest in the group. One comparatively young graduate had his own gallery — and very rich parents as Torrey learned the next day. Another had scored what sounded like a pretty interesting job as agent for an international art auction firm but positions like that were rare, and because of the need to travel in the Middle and Far East, they invariably went to males. Several graduates had taken second degrees and two had earned doctorates but the overwhelming majority, most of them around Torrey's age, were in roles with elevated titles that invariably began with "assistant to." More than anything else, this latter group reinforced Torrey's decision to become a thief.

Over the next ten years that decision paid handsome dividends. In the first place, she used her education wisely and effectively. Torrey had been a good student. She did her assignments, never skipped class and always opted for the "extras" that the faculty offered. As a consequence, she knew her stuff. Not only did she know art — oil paintings and watercolors were her particular favorites — she knew what would sell. Better than that, she knew what would sell even if it was — sometimes *because* it was — hot.

To the skills she had learned, Torrey added several natural gifts. She was, by her own description, if not plain, then at least ordinary looking. "Average, average, average" was the phrase she used to summarize her appearance. Nothing about her attracted attention. It was an important reason why, despite her relative youthfulness, she was always readily accepted as a cleaning lady. The same body that allowed her to go unnoticed was also a sound and healthy one. It took more than a little strength, for example, to balance on the edge of a bathtub at the Montag residence — where she took the Picasso — and stretch to cut a square out of the screen with a box cutter. Reaching the window of the downstairs bathroom in that wing of the house was an awkward stretch.

Another valuable gift was patience. The dealer in Seattle who specialized in Canadian art was a case in point. He and his wife had oils all over their house but Torrey waited for more than a year before successfully lifting an Emily Carr from their dining room. Patience had worked for her too at the faculty club in Eugene. Right away she had seen the University of Oregon campus was shockingly slack with its security, and it was oh-so-tempting to scoop and run. Yet she had dutifully mopped and scrubbed and dusted through the very slow spring and summer semesters, knowing that the frenetic pace of the first weeks of fall term — when she scored a small Winslow — would bring hordes of bodies through the faculty club, making it almost impossible for the police to trace everybody's movements.

Still another trait worked in her favor. Torrey was not greedy. At the Gelfs' mansion in Sacramento she'd had a choice of Riopelles, one of Torrey's favorite artists. The Gelfs were mad about the moderns and their collection was huge. So big, in fact, that the Riopelle she took wasn't even missed until a tax accountant had insisted on taking inventory and doing a general re-evaluation. That was because Torrey's pick was modest and, if it could be called so, almost discreet.

After a decade of deliberate, almost plodding thievery, Torrey had amassed a small fortune; not a huge one for that would be out of character and inconsistent with her master plan. Still, she was quite ready now to take the next step. She'd always wanted to spend time in Tahiti, resting on the beach, idling in the waters of a lagoon, perhaps discovering what it was that appealed so to Gauguin when he turned his back on France to live there. Thus it was that, here at the Montags', she decided to make her most ambitious, and last ever, lift: a Picasso.

The approach was true to form. She'd been cleaning for months now at the Montags', long enough to become part of the woodwork as so typically happened in wealthy households. The Picasso she had her eye on was from the famous "Blue Period," not a knockout canvas that even the I-know-what-I-like school of art appreciation would know, but rather — and typically — a piece that could be fenced with some ease but which, because of the signature, would fetch a tidy sum.

The Montags' security system was no child's play. Still, Torrey had needed only a few weeks to discover how to get around it. That was necessary this time because she had decided on a break-and-enter diversion. Not her first choice of method if only because this was to be her last ever theft, her "pension" as she'd begun to think of it. In fact, because there would be no more steals and because she would be leaving for Tahiti anyway — using one of her several identifications — Torrey had seriously considered just leaving at the end of a cleaning day with the stolen painting in a bag hanging from her shoulder, and after meeting with her fence, going straight to the airport. However, there were details from previous activities that still needed her personal attention here in Los Angeles. Together with the fact that the Montags were away for the month and that her fence was still negotiating with the buyer of the Picasso, she decided to stick around for a while and make the theft look like an ordinary break-in. The challenge did not intimidate her as she had managed this several times before.

Cutting the screen in the bathroom window was something she'd left until late morning on what she called "L-Day" (Lift Day). The week before, confident it would never be noticed until investigators made a detailed search, she had rewired the window's security so that it would appear modified from the outside. The tamper-proof feature of the system had given her a bit of a run, but as with everything else she did, patience brought success. Then, at the beginning of her lunch hour on L-Day, she carefully lowered the Picasso on a sling to the flower bed below, completely at ease because she knew she was the only person who ever came to this part of the house when the Montags were not in residence. Then, being careful to leave her fingerprints on the door knob — she *was*, after all, the cleaning lady — but not on the sink or toilet because that's where she wore rubber gloves, and certainly not anywhere on the sill, Torrey brought the window down to just within a crack of fully closed, and went out to the yard to eat her lunch.

The period between her lunch break and 4 p.m. on L-Day was the only time she felt nervous because for several hours the Picasso would be resting in her bag. This was, she felt, the only time when coincidence or bad luck could trip her up. Everything else had been planned and accounted for. She'd waited that morning at the rear entrance, as she had for months, while Euphoria, the Montags' full-time maid, had turned off the security system and let her in. At noon she went into the south yard as she always did without fail every day to eat her lunch. She ate at a little table near a pond garden, the only part of the yard where neighbors, if they bothered to, could see into the Montag property. And after eating, bag over her shoulder, Torrey went for her regular, languid stroll around the yard, a sojourn that, every day, took her past the bathroom window.

Below the window, secure in the knowledge she could not be seen, but acting swiftly nevertheless, Torrey slipped the Picasso from behind some blooming wisteria into her bag, careful to step only on the brick chips in the flower bed. She then took a slightly worn man's Nike from her bag and made a partial footprint on a patch of earth near the wisteria. After two more circuits of the yard, again a customary habit, Torrey returned to the house where she noted with relief that Euphoria was having her usual noon hour snooze.

On her way home the evening of L-day, Torrey delivered the Picasso, dropped the Nike into a garbage bin miles from the Montags', and finally settled into an easy chair with a very large, very dry, martini. Next week, on her regular clean, she would notice that the Picasso was gone and ask Euphoria if she knew why it had been moved. It was not likely that the screen would even be noticed until the theft was reported and a thorough investigation begun. The steady but simple cleaning lady the Montags had employed for the better part of the past year would answer questions of course, but really, what could she be expected to know about anything?

Despite her careful, deliberate planning, Torrey has made one mistake that could draw suspicion toward her. What is that mistake?

Solution on page 185

31

The New Recruit

A local wag running for town council in Serenity once remarked, only half in jest, that a better name for the place would be "Stability" since nothing ever changed. He was defeated in the ensuing election, not so much because of his poorly thought out comment but because of his origins, for this would-be councilor was "from the city." Despite having lived in the community for almost 20 years, and notwithstanding that over that time he'd taken a dying retail store and turned it into the town's most popular and successful enterprise, being "from the city" was simply too large an obstacle to overcome when standing for municipal office in Serenity. Curiously, his wife topped the polls in the voting for the school board even though she, like her husband, had only lived in the town for 20 years. Unlike her husband, however, she had been born and raised in a small town. To the good citizens of Serenity, that qualification minimized the risk.

It was a keen awareness of this cultural phenomenon that shaped Staff Sergeant Elmer Farrell's thinking when he put in a request to headquarters in Regina for a constable to work in Serenity under cover. Elmer specified that the constable had to be, absolutely and clearly, a "small town type" with all the sensitivity to nuance and understanding of local values that this implied. Elmer's superiors at headquarters, almost all of them his contemporaries, were flabbergasted by the request and, at first, they simply ignored it. In their view, nothing — as in *nothing* — ever happened in Serenity, illegal or otherwise. Indeed, Elmer had been posted there as a reward for long service, the thought being that he would spend his few remaining pre-retirement years if not dozing, then, at least in peace. However, when Elmer, an aging cop all right but no slouch, provided incontrovertible evidence that Serenity hosted one of the largest and most sophisticated marijuana growing operations the RCMP had ever encountered, the request for help moved ahead with remarkable speed.

At the moment, the product of that bureaucratic burst of speed, Special Constable Harry Smithers, was leaving a variety store on Main Street where it intersected Church Road. Elmer had watched Smithers pull up to the store in his battered green pickup, go inside and then come out with a pack of cigarettes. (Although Elmer had not specified "smoker" in the qualifications, the fact that Harry Smithers either had the habit or else took it on as a duty was a definite plus. For reasons not hard to figure, there was no anti-smoking legislation in Serenity. It had been proposed once, by the head of the Downtown Improvement Association, another person "from the city," but even the church groups had turned thumbs down.)

Smithers had exited the variety store after less than a minute, popped the lock on his pickup, got in and lit up. Normally, the brevity of the stop would have bothered Elmer. In a small town you don't just go into a store, buy something and walk out. You chat a bit, ask about the kids, talk about the weather, stuff like that. But this particular variety store owner wasn't just "from the city"; he was new and "from away," some Asian country. It would be a while before locals engaged in conversation in this store.

Elmer took a step farther back into the shadows beside Annie's Gas 'n' Go. It was a favorite observation spot from which he could watch just about the whole of Main Street without being seen. Yet the new recruit's next move was such a good one that Elmer couldn't help wonder whether Smithers had spotted him. What the young man did was start his truck, and then without hesitation *and* without signaling, make a U-turn and proceed back up Main the way he'd come. Half a block on he stopped at the coffee shop, the rear wheels too far from the curb.

Elmer stared for a long moment and then backed farther into the shadows until he could go into Annie's by the side door. He'd have his coffee break here. In his opinion, Annie made a better brew than This Pot's 4 U and besides, he didn't want to be seen in the same place as Harry Smithers any more than would seem normal in a town the size of Serenity. Annie talked to him easily too, unlike her fellow citizens. As a cop he was used to isolation and it didn't bother him that he'd never be embraced in Serenity. But as a cop it did bother him that he would never be able to penetrate the marijuana grow-op without someone at ground level, so to speak. Oh, he could shut down the growers all right; he already knew where two of them were and had a handle on three more. But the reason he had to get someone inside — not all that terribly hard if you were local, or perceived to be sufficiently small town — was to uncover the bigger fish controlling the whole thing.

Whether Harry Smithers was the right man or not ... well, Elmer just didn't feel comfortable. The credentials proclaimed him as born and raised a country boy, and all his RCMP postings so far had been rural and Far North. But Elmer knew that headquarters didn't do deep background probes for temporary assignments like this. And if it worked out, if they successfully rousted the grow-op right up to the top guys, then the undercover man's personnel file — Harry Smither's — would look really good. In a slow-to-promote force like the RCMP that counted. The only thing was, Elmer said to himself, Harry sure acted small town, but sometimes he ... well, take that terrible mistake he made out there on Main Street.

What did Harry Smithers do that was definitely not "small town"?

Solution on page 185

32

The Secret Service at Work

The man in everyday civilian clothes, standing in the fog at the edge of the cobblestone street, was a centurion recently detached from the 20th Legion. His name was Marcus Laponius Trebo. Unlike most of the centurions in the province of Britannia he was not a Roman, at least not technically, for he was born in Gaul. But Trebo had been in Britannia for most of his military career and was a veteran of the recurring tribal rebellions against the Empire's occupying forces. He thought like a Roman now and he acted like one.

Twenty years before, as a newly arrived foot soldier, Trebo had marched out of Londinium with the rest of his legion, abandoning the provincial capital and leaving its residents to be slaughtered by Queen Boadicea and her ferocious Iceni clan. And not long after, he'd stood in the front ranks as Boadicea foolishly marched her troops into a trap that cost the lives that day of thousands of her warriors, as well as their families that, in supreme over-confidence, had come out to watch. In the time since, Trebo had fought the Brigantes in the north, the Trinovantes in the east, and the fanatical Silures in the west. He'd been part of the suppression of the

Druids, stood guard duty during the development of Britannia's profitable lead mines and, just recently, endured three months of daily seasickness on the ship that finally proved what many in Rome had long suspected: that Britannia is an island.

For his loyalty and steadiness, Trebo had earned his way to what all his colleagues felt was the front of the line for someone not born a Roman. Centurions were the backbone, the sergeant-majors of the most successful army the world had yet known, both as conquerors and as occupiers, and promotion to this rank was not given lightly. And it seemed that the gods had yet another adventure for Trebo, because immediately after the successful circumnavigation of the island province, he was summoned to headquarters. Although the 20th Legion was soon to be sent north to Caledonia, the new governor, Julius Agricola, had another role for him to play. Trebo had been chosen to head a new agency at headquarters in Londinium. He was going under cover.

While the situation in Britannia could hardly be called peaceful, there had been some gradual change. Whereas governors of this remote Roman province had once behaved like the conquerors they were, more recent appointees were trying to convince the population that accepting and supporting the Empire paid bigger dividends than opposing it. This initiative, combined with the fact that a generation of native Britons and Celts had now grown up with the Roman occupation had created a widespread, if somewhat uneasy, calm. Trebo's new job was dealing with the uneasy part.

Rome's enemies in Britannia had turned away from mass armed struggle toward smaller-scale but no less effective methods — like assassinating imperial officials. Although these worthies were regularly surrounded by a Praetorian Guard, Governor Agricola was well aware that such protection can be penetrated easily if an assassin is willing to sacrifice himself. Besides, when an occupying force is engaged in a charm offensive, a ring of guards makes for bad optics. That's why Marcus Laponius Trebo and a small, hand-picked group now worked in the shadow world of espionage and counter-intelligence. It also explained why Trebo was standing on the street this day in a cold, morning fog.

Later in the day, whether the sun came out or not, Julius Agricola and select members of his entourage would be making an official pass down the street. Normally, this was the busiest street in Londinium. Early in the day — not yet; it was barely dawn — two lines of cart traffic would flow down to the market by the river. About mid-morning and for the remainder of the day, the carts would be replaced by constant streams of chariots and mounted messengers, while both sides of the street filled with buskers, hucksters and gawkers, for the street led from the governor's residence and administration center at one end to the money exchange at the other. No thoroughfare in the province carried more important business.

Traffic would be blocked at both ends to allow for the governor's pass. He'd be on foot — part of his new, friendlier, more highly visible style. Right here where Trebo was standing, and especially on the other side where a large statue of former Emperor Vespasian on horseback dominated the streetscape, the crowds would be thick. It was a popular spot.

The sturdy centurion looked across to the statue just becoming visible now in the slowly dissipating fog. If their informant was telling the truth, that's where the assassin would be waiting, but the tip, like all information that had to be paid for, was not solid enough to provide certainty. Failing to concentrate guards here could lead to disaster, but they would take up space intended for the townsfolk, and their presence in large numbers would dilute the purpose of the official walk and be a pretty visible indication that the Romans' own belief in a new, peaceful relationship was dicey at best. As it was, there were only so many guards Trebo was allowed to place along the entire route. Optics again. And if he posted more of them here at the statue, it could mean weakening the line at other points.

Trebo peered across the street more intently. He was standing right where the informant said he'd been yesterday at noon when he overheard two men at the statue discussing an assassination plot. The centurion's experienced military eye told him precisely where extra guards could be placed to provide the best protection. The question remained, however: should they be?

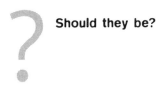

Should they be?

Solution on page 185

33

The Next Step

The Cops:
Giancarlo Bettellini, detective second grade, homicide division, aged 32. In his second year with the division, currently qualifying for upgrade to detective inspector.

Morton W. Schultz, captain, homicide division, aged 57. Three months from retirement.

The Victim:
Kevin Strath-Willis, aged 44. Sculptor of moderate fame and success, specializing in large abstract bronzes in the style of Henry Moore.

The Crime:
Homicide. Strath-Willis is found in his loft apartment on Queen Street West by his cleaning lady. He has been stabbed in the back of the neck.

The Dialogue:

In Captain Schultz's office at 3 p.m., the day of the murder.

Schultz: Yea? Who ...? Oh Betty! Yea, come in. I been waiting for you. That sculptor ... Straight or Strat something. One of those double names.

Bettellini: Strath-Willis, Kevin Strath-Willis.

Schultz: Yea, that's it. So whaddaya got, Betty? Sit down, sit down.

Bettellini: Forty-four year old white male, unmarried. Cleaning lady comes in at 8:30 a.m. every Tuesday and Friday. She called it in at 8:31. There was a saved message on his voice mail from a Brett Racine came in at 9:40 last night. He ... er ... Strath-Willis called Racine back at a few minutes to midnight. So he got taken out sometime between midnight and 8:30 this morning. ME says her best guess for now is between 1 a.m. and 2 a.m.

Schultz: What about this Racine?

Bettellini: Alibi's tight. He ...

Schultz: I was gonna ask if he thinks anybody was in the apartment there with this Strath ... Wills? ... *Willis!*

Bettellini: He's not sure, Racine. Thinks maybe, but then that could be 'cause there were often people there. Always men according to the neighbors.

Schultz: So he's one of those, whaddayacallit ... alternative lifestyles?

Bettellini: Seems so.

Schultz: And one of these visitor guys is likely the killer? A spat, maybe?

Bettellini: Could be. Almost for sure the vic ... er ... Strath-Willis knew the killer. Door was locked. Cleaning lady said she had to use her key. The vic was slumped over this fancy writing desk at the window opposite the door. Looks like he was sitting there writing when the perp nailed him in the back of the neck. Really ugly way to go.

Schultz: Don't repeat this outside my office but that sounds like the kind of thing a woman would do.

Bettellini: Yes ... er ... yes ... but she'd have to be pretty strong to put the knife in back there. Either way, I'm certain it's someone he was familiar with. Not likely he'd turn his back to a stranger. Not in his own apartment.

Schultz: You say he was writing? At this desk?

Bettellini: I think he was going on vacation or was planning to. Maybe with the perp. Here — this was on the desk. That's blood on the corner.

Schultz: After 35 years I can recognize blood, Betty. Pretty fancy paper this!

Bettellini: Whole apartment's like that. Antiques, fancy stuff.

Schultz: Mmm ... This number here, that's American Airlines, isn't it? Yea, seems like a vacation, don't it? "Arrive Grenada in p.m. at Point Salines Airport. On to Cinnamon Hill Resort and Beach Club." Guy must watch his cash. Says here the taxi into the capital, St. Peter's, is 30 bucks. Musta got that from the travel agent.

Bettellini: More likely the internet, be my guess.

Schultz: So what else you got 'sides this note?

Bettellini: I'm meeting the scene techs at 4. There's fingerprints all over. Glasses, walls, bathroom mirror. Could be a bit of a job getting matches though. Like the neighbors said, there were all kinds of guys in there all the time.

Schultz: Men he knew?

Bettellini: I don't know. He's big into the art world so my guess is there'd be all kinds of different people around; I'm thinking agents and buyers and so on. See, he's got a studio on the floor below. Huge place. Got a forge in it, can you believe that? But like I said, I'm pretty sure it was someone he knew. There was no sign of violence in the apartment — other than him. No furniture knocked over or anything like that. Unless the ME or the fingerprint guys come up with something I missed, the way I make it is someone familiar came up behind him while he was at the desk and poof!

Schultz: Okay Betty, makes sense, but if he knows so many people you got a lotta ground to cover, so what's your next step?

Bettellini: His address book. I've got this one here from beside his phone, and there's one for his email. Gonna start with guys named George and Peter.

Why is Detective Bettellini going to "start with guys named George and Peter"?

Solution on page 186

34

The Whitsun Islands Sting

Thirty minutes before Quantas Flight 504 out of Sydney via Brisbane was scheduled to touch down at the little airport on Hamilton Island, Basil Ayton unbuckled his seat belt and stumbled down the narrow aisle to the lavatory. The mirror in the tiny cell confirmed his suspicion that a combination of jet lag, upset stomach, a headache and a very sore back made him look as bad as he felt. His adventure had begun four days earlier when a telephone call to his retreat in northern Canada jolted him out of a deep sleep. Since then, Basil had spent over 29 hours in the air in five different aircraft, making his way to the northeast coast of Australia. He was exhausted, cranky and disoriented, and a day behind the planned schedule. By this time he had also spent close to $30,000 on this venture and, although he wouldn't discover the fact for another few hours, that money — not to mention his time and effort — had been completely wasted.

The telephone call had come in at 2 a.m.

"How're yuh goin' mate?" a cheery voice had shouted into the phone while Basil tried to clear away the wisps of a comfortable sleep.

Without waiting for an acknowledgement, the voice had continued.

"Get your gear together, mate. There's treasure waitin' and you're gonna want to be first in line."

Basil forced himself out of the remaining vestiges of his slumber. "Smithey, confound it!" He had shouted too. "Don't you ever look at your watch? Or your *calendar?* It's the middle of the night here. And it's winter! Freezing cold!"

Smithey didn't miss a beat. "All the more reason to get goin' mate. Bright sunshine here. Just thinkin' of sheddin' me shirt, in fact, or maybe havin' a swim. Yuh wanna join me? And load up a pot of cash into the bargain?"

He didn't wait for Basil to reply. "Look, I got the find of the century waitin' here," he said. "You've never seen a site like it. What's that favorite word of yours — *pristine?* Well, this is pristine. It's up by the Whitsuns and it's completely intact. Nobody's ever been near it."

By this time, Basil was standing beside his bed. "Wait a minute, wait a minute, Smithey! Where are you calling from? Sydney? Cairns? And what kind of site ... it's in the Whitsunday Islands? They're a national park those islands, aren't they? That sounds like trouble."

"No, no, not right *in* the Whitsuns. It's a little chain a couple degrees north. Folks here call 'em the Boogers cause they're mostly atolls and reef crags but one of 'em's bigger. Site's on that one and mate, you gotta see it! It's ... it's ... well, remember that dig we worked on up near Darwin some years ago? Just like that one but a bit smaller. I'd say up to four, five aboriginal families at any one time, maybe as many as seven or eight generations in the settlement but the thing is it's ..." There was a long breath. "It's *fresh!* Looks like one day they just took off and left everything behind. Quake country up there y'know."

While Smithey waited for reaction, Basil tried to evaluate. The Whitsunday Islands formed a small archipelago on the eastern coast of Australia, about midway between Brisbane and Cairns, in the Great Barrier Reef. Some islands were inhabited and private; others had been turned into commercial vacation spots. It just didn't make sense that in an area as popular as the Great Barrier Reef an early aboriginal settlement, even a small one, could have gone undiscovered until now. Still, when people visited the area they came to dive and snorkel and lie on the beaches; they didn't come to roam around the islands. And one had only to think of recent archeological discoveries right underneath the streets and homes of teeming cities like Cairo and Damascus, even London and Paris, to realize that finding a pristine site near the Whitsunday Islands did not stretch the imagination.

Smithey had then broken the silence. "First trip in," he said, "we'd hardly have to dig. There's enough good stuff on the surface to turn a profit without even using a shovel."

The thought of "good stuff" waiting to be taken almost without effort was what convinced Basil to discard any thought of more sleep. Over the next several hours, he got his gear together, wired Smithey the requested advance of $20,000 on his finder's fee, canceled all his upcoming appointments and booked his flights.

Basil Ayton was a broker specializing in native art, but not the kind of specialist likely to be invited to conferences on archeology. His work was behind the scenes, servicing collectors whose passion for particular kinds of art and history encouraged them to ignore heritage and customs laws. The "good stuff" Smithey had referred to would be artifacts of aboriginal culture: weapons, utensils, carvings, children's toys, maybe even a didgeridoo. An authentic one of those could generate a bidding war, and the thought that he might come up with a "doo" in perfect condition had done much to sustain Basil throughout the long and uncomfortable journey.

When he got off the airplane at Hamilton and didn't see Smithey right away, Basil was not alarmed. After all, he had arrived much later than they'd agreed and quite possibly, even quite likely, Smithey was at the site. Still, Basil might have become a bit suspicious at the helicopter charter desk when his request for transport to "the Boogers" drew a complete blank with two agents who had no idea what or where he was talking about. But then an older gentleman had emerged from a back room in time to hear the exchange and chimed in.

"Can't fly in there, mate," he said. "No place to land. The Boogers is just mountain tops, really, peekin' outa the reef. 'Cept for one a them and it's the same, just bigger. Only way in is by boat."

At that, the only emotion Basil had room for was annoyance, but even this cooled when the older man continued.

"Anders can probably take yuh there. If he's sober. Ask for him over by the long dock, where the big launches are. If he's around, that's where he'll be."

As it turned out, Anders was indeed there. Moreover, he was both sober and willing and, within less than an hour, Basil and his gear were loaded.

"If that's all, let's be off then," Anders said, drawing a hand and long index finger across the bottom of his nose. "She's not a big boat and looks like there could be some weather soon. And we got to stop and pick up extra gas at the marina down the channel. Water too. None on the island."

It was fully an hour later, when the boat was well out on the reef that Basil realized he had been stung. Although he knew it was probably jet lag that had muddled his mind and prevented him from immediately picking up on the fraud, the realization didn't help very much.

What has led Basil Ayton to realize he has been taken?

Solution on page 186

35

One Bad Apple?

Hedley Barris slid into the single chair in front of the desk and got straight to the point. "You're not going to like this, sir," he said.

"This is Internal Affairs, Barris," Captain Lufkin replied, holding a fistful of tissues close to his nose. "We don't like anything in this department. We're not supposed to. In fact, once you start ..." He blew a stentorian honk into the wad. "Once you start liking something it probably means you're going soft. That the evidence box on the John Doe?" Another *honk*. "If you were thinking of putting it on my desk, then stop right now." *Honk.* "Put it over there on the table."

Hedley was holding a cardboard evidence box on his lap and had given no indication that he planned to put it anywhere, but Captain Lufkin had already moved to a rickety wooden table that looked like it had once done reluctant service in a high school cafeteria.

"Here on the table, Barris!" Lufkin sounded annoyed. "And put on your gloves! You touch anything belonged to this guy, you're going to end up with ..." *Honk!* "Confounded cold! He probably had all kinds of scummy diseases and the last thing you want is ... oh."

Hedley had come into the office with a pair of surgical gloves already carefully donned, but Lufkin hadn't noticed. Nor did he apologize as Hedley moved to the table and began to empty the box.

"The contents have been itemized, sir. As you can see, they ..."

"Yea, yea, of course they've been itemized. Let's just get to it. What I want to know is ... what I ... oh no, here it comes again!" With that, Lufkin served up a sneeze that reverberated into the next office, if not the next time zone.

"This is some gawdawful cold," he explained as though that was necessary, and walked back to the desk where he exchanged the wet tissues for more ammunition. Hedley, meanwhile, took advantage of the moment to empty the evidence box and back away from the table as far as he could.

"What I want to know is ..." Lufkin was still working on the sentence, "just what ..." sniff ... *sniff ... SNIFF!* "... what this guy's clothes have got to do with one of our officers digging a hole for himself. Strike that — *for all of us!* Whenever one single cop goes off the track we all get smeared. Doesn't help either that Daniels has been accused twice before of ... Oh no!"

He held up the newly acquired wad of tissue in readiness for a sneeze while Hedley took yet another step backward and held his breath, but the explosion didn't come.

"I wonder if it's this wino's clothes that's making me sneeze," the captain said, more to himself than anyone in particular, but Hedley took that as an opener to get on with it.

"He was wearing track pants, this ... er ... *street person*," Hedley said, using the end of his pen to lift an extremely dirty pair of gray athletic warm-up trousers. "In fact, he was wearing two pair. See this other pair, dark blue? And no underwear."

"Figures. Probably got them out of a dumpster somewhere. Or stole them more likely."

"I don't think so, sir. Salvation Army's been handing these out for a couple of weeks now, ever since the weather reports started predicting snow."

Captain Lufkin grunted. "Yea well, so much for the weather reports 'cause it's not snowing yet, but with how cold it's been I can see why he'd wear two." With his free hand, Lufkin used his own pen to stir various items around the table. "Socks don't match, but ... Jeez, these are better socks than *I've* got! Look brand new. Don't really need to match anyway if you're a wino. And that nice parka! This from the Army too?"

"We're checking, Captain. Some of the downtown churches have been distributing clothes to the homeless, especially since this cold snap started."

Sniff, sniff ... ah ... ah ... Honk! "Well, let me know the next time they're doing handouts. I'm going to go join the lineup. Say, where's his boots? Or shoes?"

"That's part of the issue here, Captain. See, where he was found, I mean, where his body was found ..."

"Yea, that part's in the preliminary report. Some wussy social worker swears she saw Daniels haul the Doe into his cruiser. Downtown somewhere, I forget. 4th and Pearcey? Somewhere like that?"

"On 4th, yes, in front of the Pearcey Arms. Incidentally sir, he's not quite a John Doe. We found out he goes by 'Danceman,' although that's likely a street name."

Honk! "Yea right. Danceman. What every mother would want to call her kid. And now she claims, this social worker, she's saying Daniels took Danceman for a ride. Dumped him out on the edge of town just to be mean and ... By the way, she say anything, this bleeding heart, about whether or not the wino was wearing boots?"

Hedley took a step closer to the table. "No, but that's what I meant by 'part of the issue.' Daniels says he picked him up precisely because he didn't have any and then took him over to the St. Vincent de Paul shelter."

"To get boots?"

"According to Daniels, but ..."

"Don't tell me. He didn't take him in, Daniels didn't. Just dropped him off."

"Yes, but he ..."

"Dumb."

"Well, maybe. Daniels says he would have taken him in but a 9-1-1 came through and he felt he had to respond as 'officer-nearest.'"

"Okay, that's easy enough to prove."

"Yes. The time's right and we got the record. Unfortunately the 9-1-1 was a phony. Some kids fooling around."

Lufkin peered at the soggy wad of tissues in his hand as though they held the solution. "I can write the rest of this one with my eyes closed," he said. "9-1-1 is called off so Daniels goes back to the shelter and Danceman's nowhere around, so he *assumes* the guy's in the shelter."

"That's right."

"And now we ... *sniff* ... *sniff* ... now we got a win — *street* person — who dies of exposure out on the edge of town a good four miles from the shelter, and a bleeder who says Daniels dropped him out there and Daniels himself who says the guy must have walked out there."

"That's not all."

"There's more?"

"The witness who gave us the name, Danceman ..."

"Don't tell me. Another *street person*?"

"Yes."

"Why am I not surprised? Go on."

"She says she thinks Danceman has family out there. Out in the north end where he was found."

"She *thinks.*"

"Yes."

"So that would be a reason for him to walk all the way out there and would get Daniels off the hook."

"Yes."

"Except it doesn't."

"Yes, sir, I agree. It doesn't."

 Why is Daniels not "off the hook" because Danceman may have had family near where his body was found?

Solution on page 186

36

Why Pvt. Raymond Failed

From: "Jay Polito" <jpolito@usaf.gov.us>
To: "Marty Hjadran" <mhjaran@usaf.gov.us>
Sent: Wednesday, September 28, 2009 10:05 AM
Subject: A.N. Raymond

<u>ENCRYPTED</u>

Marty,

A heads-up on Col. Bett's nephew, Pvt. Raymond. Strongly recommend you transfer him out of special ops training immediately based on error yesterday as outlined below. His application is dated 1 September so there's only two days left to wash him out without reason. That way nothing goes in his file so it may keep Bett cool.

See attached photos. (Quality's not great; lot of sun this week and I probably didn't adjust properly for light.) The concrete block building went up about six months ago, since your time in the field. Where the ammo test range used to be. Single story, more or less square as you can see, used mostly for anti-sniper work, hostage rescue, that kind of stuff. Flat terrain, not much cover in the area so it's good for training proper approaches to a hostile site (yesterday's exercise).

Photo with a check shows east and south sides. As you can see, latter has no openings, other has small window in the middle. (I know. Who builds a house with a solid wall, but this was another Pentagon idea. Apparently simulates typical low budget structures in the ME.) Other photo shows west, with a window to the right, and north side where you can see a doorway there in the middle. Roof's not quite flat, slopes just a bit north to south. Tile — no torching it like in Nam.

Raymond's assignment was to put a stun grenade inside after a covert approach on suspicion of hostiles in the building. It was a daylight approach, about this time, maybe a bit earlier, and he put the grenade through the west window.

Marty, he may be Bett's nephew but he's a road hazard! This is his *second* absolutely basic mistake in less than a week. Remember that time north of Bien Hoa when we sent that goofy kid from Boston ahead to scout a hut? Thirty-five years ago to the day next Tuesday. I don't want another day like that one and you don't either.

J.

What mistake did Pvt. Raymond make yesterday?

Solution on page 186

37

On a Grassy Knoll

The conference center was an old but graceful mansion with a history. It was built of gray stone from nearby quarries that were once the economic life of the town. The original owners had been the family that also owned the quarry but they were eventually forced to sell it to the people who put the quarries out of business. In its next life, the mansion housed a Jesuit seminary for about 40 years, after which the priests and their students were succeeded by a profoundly unsuccessful religious commune. During this latter occupation, the building became badly run down but just when it reached bottom, a hotel chain, Le Chateau Magnifique, had seen its potential and brought it back, tastefully, to its present state. The meeting of ambassadors from Europe being held there today was typical of its current use.

Large rolling lawns encircled the conference center, dotted throughout with clumps of mature oak and maple, and running around the outside edge of the 20-acre site was a tall iron fence. The fence and the compact size of the building in relation to the grounds made it ideal for security, one of the reasons it was used for high level conferences. Lisa Brockway was part of the security team for the gathering taking place today. Normally, she was Traffic Specialist Lisa Brockway, youngest and newest member of the Town of St. Mary's police department, but today she had special duty.

"You know that grassy knoll out front the Sem," Chief Davy had said, "the one to the east side the circular driveway." Long time residents still called Le Chateau Magnifique "The Sem."

Lisa replied that of course she did, she'd grown up in St. Mary's.

"That's your spot, then," the chief said. "You keep it clear. Nobody goes near but you, you hear? Not a foot goes on it but yours. You're too young, probably, to know why, but I don't want any snotty paper from the city to have even the tiniest reason for a 'grassy knoll' story. So nobody goes near and, well, naturally you watch for anything fishy no matter where you see it."

Thus Lisa was standing on the grassy knoll this morning, all by herself, feeling the early morning sun on her back and hoping it would soon dry up the dew that was making her shoes wet. She'd already been the subject of a long, lingering shot by the first TV crew to come in at dawn but she didn't really mind. She thought, mostly because the crew was all male, they were having a bit of fun. Lisa was used to being photographed, especially in her summer uniform and especially since Davy had allowed her to wear her silky blonde hair down instead of stuffed under the cap.

The crew did bother Lisa in another way, however. She didn't understand why, but they weren't shooting every single thing that moved down there at the main entrance gate. TV crews always did that but not this bunch. For example, they hadn't taken any shots of the people in the long chauffeured limo that drove up to the gate about half an hour ago, a three-seater that sped up the street, stopped at the gate and, after just seconds, with even a salute from one of the guards, moved on up the drive to the main entrance, where it immediately discharged a passenger from each of the rear and middle doors. The man who got out of the passenger side rear was obviously a conference dignitary. Had to be, the way the other passengers clustered around him. One of them, the tall woman who got out of the rear door on the driver side, practically fawned over him. Yet the TV crew had just stared. Maybe, Lisa thought, they did nothing because everything happened so quickly, for the newcomers went right inside and the chauffeur sped away the instant the doors closed. As it was, she soon had another item to attract her attention, one that she really was going to call in.

A panel truck had pulled up to the gate, stopped, and pulled right away again as soon as a tall man in blue coveralls got out. He had a holstered tool bag at his waist and a coil of wire over his shoulder. Security personnel at the gate wouldn't let him in, however, and there was quite a bit of shouting. It ended with the man crossing the street to the opposite curb where he began shouting into a cell phone. In seconds, the truck reappeared and picked him up again. Lisa figured it must have driven around the center on the perimeter road.

She had decided to label this one "fishy" but changed her mind when yet another truck appeared. This one came up the road and turned to drive in through the gate, causing a half-dozen security people to jump into the driveway in front of it. This time, Lisa was amused and it made her decide to forget about the first truck. After all, too many calls from a rookie and she'd get a reputation for crying wolf too quickly. This new arrival she recognized as a local landscaper. She even recognized the driver, the landscaper's son. Eventually, as she expected would happen, the truck was passed through and driven to the front entrance, where some potted junipers and other plants were set up on either side of the pillared entrance. For a second or two, Lisa was uneasy because she didn't know the man working with the landscaper's son but then checked herself when she reflected that in a business like theirs with such rapid employee turnover, seeing a new man, a complete stranger, was nothing unusual. And St. Mary's had been full of strangers for days now.

Just as the landscaper's truck started up again, Lisa got a hint of why the TV crew might have been inactive before. A taxi had pulled up and an elegantly dressed woman with perfect hair got out. It was the station's anchorperson. Along with her was an older lady who must have been the boss for suddenly the crew became as busy as bees. Still, it was precisely at that moment when Lisa realized that she did indeed have "something fishy" to call in, and grabbed for the squawker hanging from her belt.

What is the "something fishy" that Lisa should call in?

Solution on page 187

38

Keeping an Eye on the Docks

Like every minor official in the British colonial service, D'Arcy Frederick was expected to remain glued to his desk from sunrise to sunset. Although a modest little deck clung to the wall outside his second floor office, he was certainly not expected to use it. For a colonial servant, taking a breath of fresh air was just not done. Yet anyone looking up from the hustle and bustle of Mombassa's shabby docks on this early May morning would have seen D'Arcy not only on the deck, but leaning against the doorjamb in a manner that actually hinted at relaxation.

The colonial offices stood precisely at the end of a single lane that led up from dockside. Every cart or wagon or string of bearers or man on horseback had to head straight at the building before turning right or left to get into the city. It was a ramshackle two-story affair of rough, unpainted lumber, but unlike the structures on either side, the colonial building boasted a shingled roof, not thatch, along with what was generously called a balcony. No one, especially D'Arcy Frederick, would ever have dreamed of taking his ease on it with a cup of afternoon tea or an early evening drink. That kind of behavior was reserved for the head of service and others of equal rank. In any case, refreshments were always better served at home, never here at the dockside. The smell alone saw to that, and if not the smell, the insects.

Still, there was no question that D'Arcy Frederick was standing in plain sight this particular morning, hands in his pockets, right shoulder angled against the open door. Appearances to the contrary, he was very much on duty. D'Arcy Frederick had an eye on the docks. Behind him, just to the left of his meticulously ordered desk, the telegraph clattered away, but he ignored it as the message was the same one that came down from Nairobi yesterday, and the day before that, and the day before that. Later in the morning, if his man down on the dock came back with some useful information, he'd tap out a reply, but for the moment there was no urgency. In fact, as far as D'Arcy Frederick was concerned, here in Mombassa, stinky, frenetic and unbearably humid Mombassa, nothing ever reached the level of *urgent*. Oh, for certain it was an important port on Africa's east coast, but as far as the colonial service was concerned, and even more as far as D'Arcy Frederick was concerned, Mombassa was the back end of all backwaters.

What made that perception even harder to bear was that Europe was about to explode. It wasn't a question of whether war would come, but when — and who would fire the first shot: the Kaiser, with his mighty army? Or Czar Nicholas? Likely it would start somewhere in the fractious, uncontrollable Austro-Hungarian Empire. But *when* didn't matter to D'Arcy as much as the fact that he would be thousands of miles from the action. Sure, the German Empire had colonies — and troops — here in Africa, and yes, Kaiser Willy had expansion plans, but ...

D'Arcy shifted and took up position against the opposite door-jamb, chin up and head cocked. The telegraph had caught his attention for he recognized the somewhat amateur keying touch of his superior in Nairobi. The message was the same though: another warning to be alert for anti-colonial activity or potentially subversive action by enemies of the Empire.

Had he been certain that no one down on the dock was looking at him, D'Arcy would have made a very rude gesture at the clatter behind him, for in his opinion, Mombassa, indeed all of British East Africa was about as meaningful to the German Empire as the North Pole. But loyal servant that he was, D'Arcy kept his fingers still and his opinion to himself. Instead, he focused on a more immediate grain of sand in his shoe: assistant under-clerk Bertie Doan-Marshall, standing on the dock at the end of Pier 4. Bertie was an Australian. Not that it mattered, although D'Arcy could never quite dismiss the awareness that his assistant was not from the mother country. More important was his conviction that Bertie was an uneducated nincompoop, and the fact that he had been posted here was confirmation of Mombassa's low status in the colonial service.

Bertie Doan-Marshall's assignment on Pier 4 was to note any passengers disembarking from the *Grote Maen,* the Great Moon, a Belgian steamer that had come in on the pre-dawn tide, and make sure they completed an entry visa. D'Arcy would have preferred to be there himself, for the *Grote Maen* was captained by a dubious character named Jan Hollert who plied the coastal trade from Cairo through the Red Sea, down the coast as far as Dar-es-Salaam and back. However, among Bertie's several shortcomings was his lack of Morse code training, which meant that D'Arcy had to stay in the office by the telegraph.

Only after he'd watched the Australian confront three passengers who'd come down the *Grote Maen*'s rickety gangway, a middle-aged couple and a girl, did D'Arcy become as relaxed as he appeared. Even so, he didn't leave the doorway until it was clear the husband — he assumed it was the husband — was cooperating with the paperwork.

D'Arcy was at his desk when Bertie came up the stairs.

"Seen them, did yuh, mate?"

D'Arcy returned a cold stare until the light dawned for Bertie.

"Sorry!" he added quickly. It was taking Bertie a while to understand that "mate" had no place in the vocabulary of the colonial service.

"'Ere it is then, the visa. Hollert's out on th' tide tonight, but the passengers is stayin' here in the 'Bassa,' they are, for a while anyway."

Bertie reached between his legs to adjust himself but D'Arcy missed the move for he was studying the penmanship on the visa.

> *"Austin Bradley and two dependents:*
> *wife Justine, daughter Daphne"*

filled the first line with a calligraphic elegance he didn't often see in Mombassa. For several long moments, D'Arcy didn't even realize Bertie was still talking.

"Bit of a toff, I'd say, but decent enough. A p'fessuh. Daughter'll be a looker in a coupla years I'd say. They been down in the 'Dar' a long time. Got a year's leave now so it's back 'ome to Blighty. Goin' on to Nairobi first. Seems the missus got family there ..."

D'Arcy scanned down the overlong visa form and first noted confirmation of the academic claim:

> *" Professor of Rhetoric: Headmaster, Corydon Academy,*
> *Dar-es-Salaam,"*

and the reason for travel:

"Medical leave; affects of malaria."

Bertie meanwhile had returned to his speculations on the potential beauty of the daughter but D'Arcy heard none of it, focusing completely on the now silent telegraph key. For the first time since coming to Mombassa he was feeling a mild frizz of excitement. Unconsciously, with thumb and forefinger curved, he began tapping out a message on his knee. It had to be phrased just so. Nairobi would definitely be interested in this one.

D'Arcy Frederick is suspicious of Austin Bradley. Why?

Solution on page 187

39

To Praise a Rookie Cop

"Look. You're not getting it."

"Don't tell me I'm not *getting* it! What's not to *get*? One of my rookies follows a set of footprints. Big deal. It's *you* that's not getting it!"

"The footprints belonged to a serial killer that murdered four people in two states and one more, maybe two, in Canada."

"*Suspected* killer. And don't say 'serial.' We don't know that for sure yet either."

"But you can't ignore an opportunity like this! The PR is just too hot!"

"PR?"

"Public relations. Stop playing dumb. Look. Need I remind you there were *two* sets of footprints leading away from that truck and the kid followed the right set. Now, at the very least you have to take your fancy braid out of the closet back there and put it on for a press conference. Even if *you* want to hold back, I can tell you that Mr. and Mrs. Joe Public are ready to hear all about this. 'Green Cop Nabs I-29 Killer.' Can't you just see the headlines! Or skip around the rookie thing if that's what you want. 'Sheriff's Dept. Bags Long Distance Killer.' That'll do it too."

"My God, you really *don't* get it, do you? Okay, okay, there's PR in this, but it's got to be done carefully. For one, you're ignoring a key point. This kid wasn't alone in making the arrest. There were at least a dozen of my people out in that gully when the arrest was made. *And* if there hadn't of been, this trucker would have made mince meat outa the kid. You've seen the guy! He's a poster boy for a motorcycle gang."

"Okay, so spread the good news around. Lay the juice on your whole department."

"What do I have to do here? Look. My department didn't do this alone. It was the state troopers in South Dakota that first put it together with the Mounties up in Manitoba that whoever was responsible for this killing spree was *A:* the same guy and *B:* a long-distance trucker and *C:* driving a semi with a broken exhaust stack. You think I'm ever gonna get any cooperation again out of other police forces if I take all the glory here?"

"All right, then ..."

"And these media weenies. On a story like this they got the mind of a flea. Don't forget I've been down this road before and got burned good too! The media like *simple*. Especially the TV types. They need something that Joe Public — who by the way is probably sitting on his fat butt with a beer, waiting for "Wheel of Fortune" to come on — they need something that Joe Public can figure out in ten seconds or less! And you know what that's gonna be? It's going to be the rookie angle."

"I still don't see what's so bad about that."

"That's the trouble with you. You've never been in the trenches. What do you think is going to happen to morale in the department if this kid gets the glory?"

"Well, they'll rag 'im a bit, of course."

"More than that. If you're a guy — or a gal — say, three years in and last night you got into the middle of a domestic. Got your shins kicked, maybe scratched, spit on for sure. How're you gonna feel when the whole county is singin' about some greenhorn who's never even seen a husband and wife go at it? They don't send reporters to domestics, you know. Unless somebody gets killed and then we're in the tank for not intervening soon enough."

"Okay, why don't you present it as a shining example of intra-department, inter-force cooperation?"

"In*ter?* In*tra?* God, I can see Joe Public's eyes glaze over from here! Okay, look. I agree there's some good PR here but we've got to be one step ahead. What we have to do is *give* them the angle. They're going to do the rookie thing no matter what, but somehow ... See, there's so many parts to this. Like who was the other guy in the cab — the other set of footprints that went in a different direction? Why'd they abandon that big semi — or maybe they didn't abandon it? It wasn't damaged very badly. And what made him drop a wheel onto the shoulder so he creams up against that rock cut? In the middle of nowhere. I mean, the guy's been driving, what, 20 years or more?"

"I think maybe I've got an ..."

"Let's face it. There's a barrel of luck in this too. The kid wasn't supposed to be on patrol this morning. He wasn't even supposed to be on duty but he'd switched a shift. And what does he do? He turns off I-29 and goes down the secondary 'cause he needs to take a leak — put *that* in the press release — and boom, there's the semi everybody's lookin' for!"

"My turn, okay? I said, *maybe* I've got an idea here. The angle, I mean. How many times have you said that luck's got a lot to do with an investigation?"

"Yes, but ..."

"But *luck,* you always add, means nothing — absolutely zip — unless good solid police work rides on top."

"That's true ..."

"So here's the angle. Trust me, the media will use it. Rookie cop

— no, strike that — *sheriff's deputy,* alone on routine patrol, discovers abandoned vehicle of possible serial killer — okay, maybe not serial — and must choose which tracks to follow. How does he know which set of tracks is most likely to be the killer?"

"Because ... yes, the set that ... By God I think that's it!"

?

How does the rookie cop know which set of tracks to follow?

Solution on page 188

40

One Small Favor Before the Wedding

The room was a gloomy one, functional and cold. When it was empty, as was the case most of the time, its most obvious feature was a large, metal, overhead door, painted gray like the rest of the place. The door was never left in the "up" position and was only opened when hearses or ambulances arrived with their melancholy cargos. Opposite the door and touching the ceiling, for the room was below grade, a single tiny window offered a limited view of a parking lot. Except for about a ten-minute period on bright days, when a sliver of space between the two towers next door allowed a shaft of early morning sunlight through the bars on this window, the room was bathed in cold fluorescent light.

On this particular morning, sunlight bounced very briefly off a small diamond ring on the hand of a woman standing beside a gurney in the center of the room. She was wearing green scrubs but no mask. Her hair was uncovered and she'd not taken off her street shoes. Her name was Samantha Tapp, and although her official title was Assistant to the Coroner, anyone who knew anything at all about Peel County looked upon her as *The* Coroner. Standing on the other side of the gurney was Eddie Volkovich. His official title was Captain, Narcotics Investigation Branch, and he was one of the many who invariably turned to Samantha if there was real work to be done.

The corpse on the gurney was a male in his early 40s, although an observer might not have known that by looking at him, for the face was covered with a small white cloth. It was one of Samantha's rules for assuring dignity in death. The only other intervention, except for the syringe that stuck out of the dead man's arm, was a body tag hanging from one toe. At the moment, it too was briefly lit up by the sun. No one would ever have commented on that in Samantha's presence for another of her rules was no jokes. Ever.

Testing those rules would have been especially counter-productive on this morning because in only a few hours Samantha was due to be married.

"Just a quick look," Eddie had begged her. And when she told him there was no way in the world she was going to do an autopsy on her wedding day — and by the way, not for the next two weeks either! — he replied that all he wanted her to do was meet him in the receiving room. They didn't even need to go into the autopsy room.

"I know it's your wedding day, Sam. I mean, I'm going to be at it too, right? Just come take a look with me. He's an OD, an overdose. Heroin, I'd give ten to one odds, but anyway, just — please — just a few minutes."

Eddie Volkovich was a full head shorter than Samantha and his slightly thickening stomach came very close to the dangling syringe every time he leaned over the body, something he did every time he spoke to Samantha.

"This guy's known to us, Sam. He's in the trade, no question about that, but he was sharp. We know he was high up in the organization but we've never come close to pinning anything on him. What we'd really like to ..."

"Well, I don't see tracks, so if he's a user ...," Samantha spoke while leaning over the body, something she found easier to do than Eddie did. "If he's a user it's not heavy. Probably what you guys would call an 'occasional.' What's that other goofball phrase, 'recreational user'? 'Course we can usually get a better handle on that in an autopsy."

She straightened as though suddenly realizing what she'd said. "But I am *not* ..."

"I know, I know!" Eddie held up both hands in surrender position and then reached for the small cloth sack tied to the head of the gurney. "Take a look at this stuff," he said, "what he had on him," and began to lay the contents on the dead man's chest, being careful not to look at Samantha for he knew this was definitely playing with her rules.

There was a nail clipper, which he placed on the chest just below the dead man's chin. This was followed by a pair of glasses in thin black frames. Both ear pieces appeared to be chewed, and the right arm was taped at the hinge. Next came a ballpoint pen. It too was chewed at the end. As he brought out the next item, Eddie looked up at Samantha.

"Now, you ever see this before, Sam?" he asked. "On a druggie? I mean, in his *pocket*? It was in his shirt pocket actually. Look, it's ready to go!"

"It's an Epi-Pen, Eddie."

"A what?"

"An Epi-Pen. Mostly you see kids carrying one. It's for extreme allergies. Usually to nuts. Sometimes insect stings."

Eddie looked clearly disappointed as he returned to the cloth bag and brought out a thin wallet and laid it on the dead man's stomach. This was followed by a money clip holding what looked like a large number of folded hundreds and fifties. Samantha took a close look at it.

"Well," she offered, "whoever did in your man here didn't have robbery as a motive."

Eddie frowned ever so slightly, his fingers squeezing absently at the now empty cloth sack.

"You're thinking murder," he said. "Not overdose?"

Samantha nodded slowly. "Not much doubt. Oh, I don't think there's any question he died from whatever was in that syringe, but he didn't do this to himself."

Before Eddie could say anything, Samantha took off her scrubs and laid them gently beside the body.

"I'm due at the hairdresser, like, ten minutes ago. If you want to talk more you can come with me." She started to walk away, knowing her long strides would force Eddie to move at quick-march to keep up. "Besides, you look like you could do with a trim. Maybe a shampoo and set too since you're coming to the wedding."

Why does Samantha believe the dead man has been murdered instead of dying from a self-inflicted overdose?

Solution on page 188

Solutions

1   Alone on the Beach
What makes Tony Sanchez say that?

If the man he calls Mr. Micawber was known to be fastidiously polite, he would definitely have stood up as a lady approached his chair. The victim's footprints show him approaching the chair, sitting in it with his feet above the surface, and then not getting up again.

2   Border Alert
Which one of the three border crossers had lied to Larkin?

The man who showed the driver's license from the province of Quebec, Larkin noted, had too pale a complexion to tell whether or not a mustache had recently been shaved off. However, he said he had been hiking in the White Mountains of New Hampshire for the past week. Since the weather has been sunny and hot for more than the past week, any hiker, even one with a hat, would have become tanned or sunburned sufficiently to alter a pale complexion.

3   Homicide at 24 North Bleaker Street

In this pair of interviews there is a clue that should convince Detective Inspector Mirakawa to probe deeper. What is that clue?

Faith Orenda states emphatically that she does not know Jolene Werner ("Never heard of her"). Yet with equal emphasis she says, "What does an old lady know from blonde hair?" In the course of the interview, Detective Inspector Mirakawa never revealed that Mrs. Werner is an old lady, so how would Faith know this?

4   In Pursuit of Deserters

How does Julian Mainbridge know that the woman lied to him?

Julian is required to be in uniform at spit and polish level even when on field duty. He is also required to attend dinner in the officers' mess. Since he has only one uniform, he will do his best to keep it clean or at least presentable. If it has been raining for the past three days, and if deserters had been coming to the barn to sleep in the loft each night, there would be mud on the rungs of the ladder. In that event, Julian would not choose such a place to sit.

5   Count to Five, Press the Button and Get Out!

Did Lumpy earn his money?

Lumpy did everything right but one: he had the wrong escalator. The "suits" had told him to press the button five steamboats after he saw the guard on the *up* escalator. Unfortunately, Lumpy was watching the *down* escalator. A store hangs a sign over the bottom of a down escalator so as customers descend they know what departments they are about to encounter. A store does not hang a sign over the bottom of an up escalator as customers would have their backs to it. A hanging sign in the *up* case would be at the top of the escalator.

6   The Case of the Open Safe
What did Lassiter do wrong?
The safe is in the southeast corner of the office. From the upper floor of the warehouse across the alley, Lassiter could see everything that was in it when Barney opened the door wide. Therefore the door must face the alley (south) wall. The doorway from which Lassiter "discovers" the robbery and shouts that the safe door is open and the cash drawer is gone is diagonally across on the northwest corner of the storeroom. In the doorway, Lassiter would be able to see the safe door was open, but from that perspective he could not see that the cash drawer was gone.

7   Getting to the Front Door
Why do the jewel thieves want to wait for a warm night?
The thieves have all their bases covered except for getting the past the dogs. Since the latter are trained not to bark and to hold their capture by grabbing onto clothing, the thieves will undress and go in that way. That's why getting in, according to the "inside man," is preferable on a warm night.

8   Leave No Trace
If Moira wishes to leave no trace of herself, there should be one more item in the tote bag. What is that?
Jacques Ste-Lowe's daily calendar or date book. If he was the supremely organized type who always made lists, then he certainly would have recorded their dinner date, as well as other dates.

9   A Great Future in Art Forgery
Blaine has detected a flaw in the painting that is either a joke or an error. What is the flaw?
The duplicated "blue boy" has two left gloves. The one on the ground

lies palm up on the subject's left. The thumb is under the brim of the hat so that makes it a left glove. On the log, partly covered by the cane, is the other glove. The embroidery is visible so it must be lying palm down, and since the thumb is pointing toward the subject's left elbow, it too is a glove for the left hand.

10   A Rush Order
What does Edna expect her strategy to achieve?
The question will make many, if not most, people reflexively touch a pocket or purse or waist pack to be certain the dropped passport is not theirs. As an experienced and accomplished pickpocket, Edna will therefore be able to identify a potential client — or several. (Choosing the arrivals level for her ploy increases her chances too. Passengers are tired and far less wary after a flight than before, especially after international flights to New Zealand which, necessarily, are long ones.)

11   Undercover with the Black Lasers
What led Arnie to suspect George?
No farm boy, or anyone who claims to have rural roots for that matter, lets a tap run while he brushes his teeth. Farm boys are raised in homes with wells and cisterns as the sources of water and never ever waste it in that way. Even in homes fortunate enough to have a "good well," the tap is not allowed to run wastefully because to pump the water under pressure requires an expensive energy source, such as electricity.

12   Deadly Treasure Hunt
Culver understands that the initial numbers are a sequece beginning at 77, followed by 49, 36, and then 18. What is the next — the missing — number?
8 (Eight). The sequence is a multiplication string: 7 x 7 = 49; 4 x 9 =

36; 3 x 6 = 18; 1 x 8 = 8. The obscure measurements (not to the maker of the map, we assume) convert in more popular measure as follows.

A *rod* is 16½ ft (or 5.03 m); a *furlong* (still used in some horse racing styles) is 221 m (or 220 yd.); a *fathom* (used primarily to measure depth of water and still used by some seafarers) is 6 ft. (1.83 m); a *chain,* once an important measure in surveying, is 30.5 m (100 ft.); a *cubit* is a truly ancient unit of length describing the distance from one's elbow to the tip of the middle finger (but whose?!) around 20 in. or 50 cm. A *yard,* or .9144 m is still in use albeit, like most imperial measurement, in decline.

A *nautical mile* is 1852 m (2026 yd.) while a *statute mile* is 1925 m (1760 yd.).

13   Too Much Medication?
Why does Marissa believe there is evidence of a crime here?
Mrs. Panadopolos is 78 years old with diabetes and arthritis. She lives alone and is dead in her bed. Marissa Brezlaw lies face down to reach under the bed for the pill bottle. To do that, she must lie flat and full length. As she gets out from under the bed, Marissa tangles one foot in Mrs. Panadopolos's walker and knocks it over. Assuming Marissa is of normal adult height, this means the walker was situated well away from the bed. An old lady who lives alone and uses a walker would not place it far from her reach upon retiring. It was moved by someone after the old lady got into — or was put into — her bed. That, in Marissa's opinion, needs investigation.

14   Detective Aylmer's Report
What is the "hole" in Blackburn's story?
Detective Aylmer is proceeding along Talliser Drive West when he receives the call but is diverted south. He then goes west again and then north back up to Talliser to get to 8788 Talliser West. Therefore

he was traveling west on Talliser. The main front entrance was locked, so he accessed the building from a shipping dock at the rear, on the north side. Thus the main entrance faces south. Blackburn's office is in the middle of the building on the second floor above the main entrance, so it faces south. At 10 to 11 a.m. on a clear sunny day, the sun will be shining *into* the windows of that office. Blackburn would not be able to see a reflection in the windows under conditions like that.

15   An Impulse Rewarded

Will Melody's discovery support the veracity of the newer will or the older one?

The older will. The note supports the newer will by making it appear that Jason Corby was still alive on May 22, the day *after* the date of the new will. But because the note is fraudulent, it will certainly erode any claims for the veracity of this second will.

Melody notes the dampness in the root cellar, dampness that prevailed in her first visit on May 28, and is still present "six, seven months" later (the words of her sergeant). That dampness, along with the moisture from tulip bulbs that have been dug out of the earth and stored in the bag on the same day, would have softened the paper considerably so that Melody could not flick it with her fingernail. It is also very likely that as the paper absorbed moisture the ink would have run, so that "dug out & stored May 22 a.m." would not be clear. It appears someone placed this note so it could be discovered at an appropriate time.

16   A Second Opinion on the Case

Why do both Vera and Ivor conclude that R. Guilford Ferren's death is not a suicide? How did Vera's "woman's eye" contribute to that conclusion? Why does Ivor determine that the killer is

not a stranger but, at the same time, not someone who knew Ferren well?

R. Guilford Ferren is shot in the right temple. Had his death wound been self-inflicted — with a gun — it is far more likely the wound would have been in the left temple for he is left-handed. A right-handed man would not have his desk lamp on the right side of the desk (and likely not a box of tissues either, for they would add clutter where he needs space).

Vera's "woman's eye" noted the nearly obsessive neatness in the room. Although it is only speculation, she believes such a person would not take his own life in such a messy way — using a gun. There are far neater ways to bring about one's end.

Because Ferren's body is slumped across the surface of the desk, Ivor concludes the shooter came around to the back of the desk or at least around to the side. If he's shot from the front of the desk, the doorway side, it is far more likely Ferren's body would be slumped back in the chair. Ferren would have allowed someone he knew to come right into the office but a person who does not know Ferren intimately (like the electrician) would not necessarily know that his intended victim is left-handed.

17   Corinne Beardsley's Deadly Mistake
What was Corinne Beardsley's deadly mistake?

Carrying a rosary in a city with a tradition of Protestantism would not have been a big deal. Nor would carrying a cloth bag have attracted unnatural attention. During the occupation, French women prowled the streets grabbing any opportunity to buy food when it appeared in the stores. And it would have been quite ordinary for someone like Corinne to cross the square on her way to Saint Pierre for the noon Angelus. But a regular citizen who trudged to the church every day to pray the Angelus would not be likely to look up when the bells ring.

Staring up at the twin spires of Ste. Étienne would attract attention. If the counter-intelligence forces feared invasion, they would be more than usually alert to that. And in this case the "citizen" is carrying explosives.

18 After Hours at the Bank
What inadvertent alarm call has the gang sounded?

It is a regular practice for the four regular overtimers on alternate Thursdays to order in from the diner at around 9 o'clock. Ollie made sure the order that went in did not trigger an alarm by asking for something way out of the ordinary. But what he could not disguise was the quantity. If the people at the diner are even a bit alert, it would cause them to question why the order is doubled this time.

19 Analyzing a DJ
Apparently Orpheus has made a mistake that leads the CSA to conclude this is a "dump" and not a "jump." What is that mistake?

If Lucinda had jumped from the third-floor balcony of her own will, she would have been alive at the time and therefore, before her body cooled it would have melted the snow underneath her (the snow was only shoe depth and wet to begin with). The perfect footprints are also an issue. Given the similar size of Orpheus and Lucinda it is illogical to conclude that he could carry her body wearing her slippers and make such perfect prints. What the CSA concludes is that he killed her and dumped her out the *second*-floor balcony. But in the time it took to move the body around, dress it in a nightgown (they'd had drinks right after coming home from the party), make footprints, put the slippers back on, clean up, etc., Lucinda's body had cooled enough so that it did not melt the snow underneath it.

20   The Anthrax Plot

Despite his careful preparation, Yuri has made at least two errors. What are they?

The watch is an obvious error that Yuri seems to have overcome, at least on the surface, for a knockoff Rolex is a reasonable enough explanation. But combined with his second mistake the explanation has added a focus. Yuri says he got the knockoff in Marseilles. Too much information. Why add Marseilles? That is another detail that may turn into a clue because it seems the guard noticed the other, more serious slip up: Yuri's hands. He went to some lengths to make sure the guard noticed *non*-bank president behavior — wiping his nose with his finger. Yuri also lifted his cap and scratched his head. Both actions drew attention to his hands, his manicured, uncalloused, bank-president hands. An alert guard would naturally pay attention to a brand new driver and, if not immediately, then on reflection, would notice the hands.

21   Assessing the Risk

Why does Penny suspect a booby trap?

There is a fire in the fireplace. A fire is unnecessary for warmth as the day is warm enough for gnats to be bothering Penny as she stands in the ditch peering through the couch grass. The grass, which is tall enough to hide her and thick enough to require parting, also confirms the season. A fire is unnecessary for cooking because the utility poles indicate the use of modern energy sources. And to reinforce her suspicion that a fire is wrong in this scenario, a windless day means even a modern chimney will function poorly. Smoke will not rise easily and can easily fill the cabin.

Penny suspects the fire is there to initiate something: likely strategically placed gasoline or other chemical set up to explode when the doors are broken down.

22   The Unlamented Demise of Tony "the Heaver" Pellino

Marisa Letto has put together information that should, at the very least, prod the police into investigating Barker Fritz-Lane more aggressively. What is that information?

Since Tony was killed on a chilly, rain-soaked afternoon, even if the pub had an outdoor patio, Barker Fritz-Lane and the waitress-girl-friend-witness would have been inside. Barker has asthma just like Tony Pellino. An asthma sufferer would be unable to spend an entire afternoon in a smoky pub.

23   A Perfect Crime?

The narrator has described his plan as "foolproof" but there is potential for glitches. What are the possible weaknesses in his perfect crime?

The potential for committing a *perfect* crime invariably diminishes when a perpetrator leaves the scene with stages in the process yet to come. There are too many things that can go wrong, especially if the crime depends upon as fickle an element as leaking gas. Yet, weak as it is, setting up a gas explosion continues to be a popular method in mystery fiction. It is weak because so much depends on the rate at which the gas leaks into the basement and subsequently into the rest of a building. In this case it's entirely possible that the rate may be too slow and combustion will not take place while the narrator can account for his being out of the house with the investment advisor, dentist and car dealer. On the other hand, if it seeps in fairly quickly, the explosion, if indeed it does occur, may draw suspicion because it will happen too soon after the narrator leaves for his appointments. Then there is the element of chance by which someone (such as the mailman) might smell the gas and report it.

A further weakness arises out of the physics of gas, air and combustion. In a controlled environment like a furnace, the gas burns according to the design of the mechanics surrounding it. In an uncontrolled environment like the TV room, it may explode incompletely, or it may simply start a fire without exploding at all. The pilot light may start things before an explosion of significant damage can occur, or it's entirely possible that static electricity in the basement may start things too early. Each of these possibilities would leave the dead wife's body in a condition whereby a forensic examination would uncover damaging evidence.

Finally, the narrator seems to have ignored the lengths to which gas companies go to reconstruct an explosion in order to uncover cause, for their very existence depends on proving their systems are safe. The narrator could well be undone by the tampered-with fitting. In a world where airplanes that crash in the ocean can be retrieved and the cause uncovered, a localized situation such as this should be an easily surmountable challenge.

24 Mr. Mayo's Wakeup Test

What was Ditzy's answer?

If the apple is cut in half, the halves are the same size and neither "bigger" nor "biggest" applies.

Aficionados of appropriate language will of course have noted here that the comparative (bigger) is used for two and the superlative (biggest) for three or more.

25 Mr. Mayo's Wakeup Test: A Sequel

What are Ditzy's answers to Mr. Mayo's three wakeup tests?

Four nines can be arranged to equal 100 in this way: 99 + 9/9.

G goes below the line, H and I above. The position is determined by the presence of curved versus straight lines.

The error on the gravestone is that Rebecca Jane Bridger could not have been Piper Thomas Mann's widow. She died on June 9, 1743, at age 84, *before* her husband who died on May 22, 1752, at age 95.

26   Leo's Interim Report

Leo still has to submit a final and more formal report, but he has concluded that Albert's death is not a suicide. Why?

Albert regularly backed out his laneway to meet Berniece Laviere so that he could get his mail as usual around 9 to 9:15 a.m. Berniece, for reasons she explains in her interview, did not show up until about 11:30. Because there has been a snowfall, and the plows regularly clear the roads real early, they would have created a snow bank at Albert's driveway. Albert is an old man in an old car and backed into that bank which would have covered — and plugged — the end of the tail pipe. By the time Berniece discovered Albert, the unusually powerful chinook would have melted away the snow so that when Constable Sabapathy arrived at the scene, the pipe would have been free of any snow. It would have been fairly straightforward for him to conclude that Albert took his own life.

27   An Enemy Within?

What logic tells Sir Guy de Taillebourg the English archer did not shoot the arrow that killed Pierre-Paul?

If the rain and mist for the past five days has made it impossible for the siege engineers to work the catapults because the ropes that wind them have been softened by dampness, that same level of humidity will have affected the string of a longbow, especially if the arrow (a.k.a. "clothyard" and "bolt") must be delivered to the edge of the weapon's range. Therefore the archer — the only one with the skill to do so — could not have launched the arrow from the parapet to kill Pierre-Paul. Quite possibly, someone stabbed Pierre-Paul with the arrow in dagger fashion so that blame would naturally fall to the archer.

28   En Route to the Scene
Calla Zentil has apparently discovered something that affects her opinion of Eva and Chuck's claim. What is that discovery?

Eva makes clear throughout the drive that they are in territory so unfamiliar to her that she appears uncertain, from time to time, about just where the accident occurred. Yet as they approach the site, she slows and pulls far to the right to go over a railway crossing. Only someone familiar with the road she's driving on and familiar with the bumps that so frequently mark rail crossings on country roads would know to do that. A stranger might slow down for a crossing but would not know that one side is smoother.

29   A Discussion at Clancy, Goldberg & Associates
What evidence has the investigator, Gerwal, provided which will enable Clancy to undermine Mrs. Moskovitz's testimony?

The gas bar — or petrol station — where Mrs. Moskovitz is apparently a regular customer is on the northeast corner of King and Queensgate. Since the lady lives just to the east, she drives west on Queensgate and enters the station from that street, or, in the photographs, from the side view. The fact that each receipt shows a carefully even amount ($20, $19.50, etc.) suggests she is served by an attendant at the station, and thus uses the full serve island. Attendants, especially with cash-paying customers, invariably round a gasoline fill to amounts like these that make money exchanges easier to calculate. Since the fuel door is on the driver's side of her Buick (the same side as the dent, or *dinger*), Mrs. Moskovitz will have pulled up to the right side of the full serve pumps. This puts her in the vehicle alley immediately in front of the station building. It also puts her in the least advantageous position to see a car go west on Queensgate into the intersection at King Street. Because she will be in her car while being served, she is facing away from the intersection. Even if she turns to look, her view of the intersection would be partially, if not fully blocked by the self-serve pump islands to her left (and, quite likely in rush hour, customers pulled up beside them). Given all this information, it should be easy for Clancy to raise doubts about Mrs. Moskovitz's testimony. It is more likely than not that she paid attention only after hearing the crash.

30   An Alternative Career
Despite her careful, deliberate planning, Torrey has made one mistake that could draw suspicion toward her. What is that mistake?
Torrey and Euphoria are the only people regularly in the house while the Montags are away so it is certain they will be examined intensely. The examination is certain to be intensified if the investigators take careful note of the screen. Because the screen has been cut from the inside, fibers at the incision will be bent outward. Someone actually breaking *in* through the window will cut the screen in a manner that presses the fibers inward. The screen in its present state will point to an "inside" job.

31   The New Recruit
What did Harry Smithers do that was definitely not "small town"?
He locked the pickup truck while he made a quick sprint into the variety store. That is very urban behavior. Even worse, Smithers knew he was going into a variety store where locals did not yet linger for conversation. If he were truly "small town" he would very likely have left the key in the ignition and the motor running too.

32   The Secret Service at Work
Should they be?
Not likely. If the informant stood where Trebo stands now, he would not have been able to hear a conversation across a cobbled street filled with chariots that have either wooden or metal banded wheels, drawn by horses. It seems the informant may well be setting a trap.

33   The Next Step

Why is Detective Bettellini going to "start with guys named George and Peter"?

It makes sense for any detective to dig deeper into what the victim was writing at the time of his murder, and Kevin Strath-Willis did indeed leave a clue. The capital of Grenada is St. George's, something he certainly would know if he can name the airport, a hotel and even the cab fare. It appears to the detective that the sculptor knew he was in danger and put a name on paper in what would likely be seen by the murderer as a normal, harmless note.

34   The Whitsun Islands Sting

What has led Basil Ayton to realize he has been taken?

If there is no water source available on the island in question, then no group of aboriginal families would have stayed there long enough to establish a settlement.

35   One Bad Apple?

Why is Daniels not "off the hook" because Danceman may have had family near where his body was found?

If Danceman had walked a good four miles wearing only socks, the socks would no longer look brand new.

36   Why Pvt. Raymond Failed

What mistake did Pvt. Raymond make yesterday?

Since there are suspected hostiles in the building, the only logical way to approach in flat terrain with little cover is from the south, toward the wall with neither a door nor window. It is safe to assume that Pvt. Raymond did that, but his error was using the window on the west wall for the grenade. J's memo was written at 10:05 a.m. and the exercise took place the day before at about that time or maybe a bit earlier. Since it was sunny that day, as it apparently has been all week, Raymond's shadow would have been cast ahead of him (to the west). Hostiles in the building would easily have been able to see Raymond's shadow in time to react before he made it to the corner and around it.

37   On a Grassy Knoll
What is the "something fishy" that Lisa should call in?
With one exception, all the activity Lisa can see from the grassy knoll is explainable. Indeed, much of it she explains to herself. But one incident is unusual and that is the chauffeur-driven limousine and its passengers. Neither the chauffeur nor the three subordinate passengers opened the door for the supposed dignitary who got out of the rear seat, passenger side. If he were important enough to be chauffeured to this conference of diplomats, someone would definitely be opening the car door for him. Even more likely, he would have been greeted at the entrance. Perhaps he is not what he seems, something that Lisa should report.

38   Keeping an Eye on the Docks
D'Arcy Frederick is suspicious of Austin Bradley. Why?
Bradley makes errors on the visa, something that D'Arcy notices immediately because the man presents himself as a professor of rhetoric. A professor of rhetoric might accidentally write "depend*ent*" instead of "depend*ant*" in the stress of the moment. (Although the ant/ent distinction is fading now in the 21st century, an educated person in Bradley's time would have used "ant" only as a noun and "ent" as an adjective. For example, one has *dependants* who are *dependent* persons.) Writing *affects* instead of *effects,* however, is an error too profound and unusual for a professor of rhetoric to make, no matter how tired or harried he may be. D'Arcy believes Bradley

is not what he says he is, and therefore might be a spy sent to report on British preparedness in Mombassa and Nairobi.

39   To Praise a Rookie Cop

How does the rookie cop know which set of tracks to follow?
Both sets of footprints will exit from the driver's side door, because the vehicle was jammed up against a rock cut. Therefore the exit door — passenger versus driver side — does not provide what would otherwise be an obvious clue. What the rookie cop must have done, however, is base his choice on the nature of the footprints. The bottom of a truck driver's footwear always tells a tale. The sole of the right boot or shoe is always worn more than the left as a consequence of constant use on the brake and accelerator.

40   One Small Favor Before the Wedding

Why does Samantha believe the dead man has been murdered instead of dying from a self-inflicted overdose?
The sunlight coming through the small window lights up Samantha's engagement ring so her left side is toward the window. It also lights up the dead man's toe tag. Therefore she is standing on his left side. (The toe tag must be to Samantha's left; otherwise her body would keep the sunlight from illuminating it.) On the other side, on the dead man's right, Eddie's stomach comes very close to the syringe that still hangs from the victim's arm: his right arm. The glasses brought out of the cloth sack have chewed ear pieces, indicating they have come off frequently to be gnawed at absently as many people do. It would appear the victim, again as many people do, took them off with one hand, his right hand, because that arm has been repaired with tape. He would do this, naturally, with his right hand because he is right-handed. Just as naturally, if he were going to inject himself, he would do so with his right hand, but he

could only do that into his left arm. Samantha feels that while there may be no doubt he died from an overdose or from an allergen in the syringe, it was administered by someone else.